Y0-BYC-109

TEACHING LITERACY IN FOURTH GRADE

TOOLS FOR TEACHING LITERACY

Donna Ogle and Camille Blachowicz, Series Editors

This highly practical series includes two kinds of books: (1) grade-specific titles for first-time teachers or those teaching a particular grade for the first time; (2) books on key literacy topics that cut across all grades, such as integrating literacy with technology and science, teaching literacy through the arts, and fluency. Written by outstanding educators who know what works based on extensive classroom experience, each research-based volume features hands-on activities, reproducibles, and best practices for promoting student achievement. These books are also suitable as texts for undergraduate- or graduate-level courses; preservice teachers will find them informative and accessible.

TEACHING LITERACY IN SIXTH GRADE
Karen Wood and Maryann Mraz

TEACHING LITERACY IN KINDERGARTEN
Lea M. McGee and Lesley Mandel Morrow

INTEGRATING INSTRUCTION: LITERACY AND SCIENCE
Judy McKee and Donna Ogle

TEACHING LITERACY IN SECOND GRADE
Jeanne R. Paratore and Rachel L. McCormack

TEACHING LITERACY IN FIRST GRADE
Diane Lapp, James Flood, Kelly Moore, and Maria Nichols

PARTNERING FOR FLUENCY
Mary Kay Moskal and Camille Blachowicz

TEACHING LITERACY THROUGH THE ARTS
Nan L. McDonald and Douglas Fisher

TEACHING LITERACY IN FIFTH GRADE
Susan I. McMahon and Jacqueline Wells

TEACHING LITERACY IN THIRD GRADE
Janice F. Almasi, Keli Garas-York, and Leigh-Ann Hildreth

INTEGRATING LITERACY AND TECHNOLOGY:
EFFECTIVE PRACTICE FOR GRADES K–6
Susan Watts Taffe and Carolyn B. Gwinn

DEVELOPING LITERACY IN PRESCHOOL
Lesley Mandel Morrow

TEACHING LITERACY IN FOURTH GRADE
Denise Johnson

INTEGRATING LITERACY AND MATH:
STRATEGIES FOR K–6 TEACHERS
Ellen Fogelberg, Carole Skalinder, Patti Satz, Barbara Hiller, Lisa Bernstein, and Sandra Vitantonio

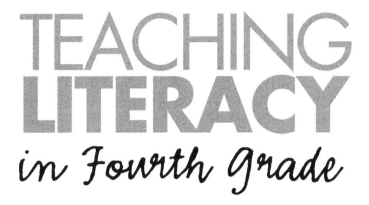

TEACHING LITERACY
in Fourth Grade

Denise Johnson

Series Editors' Note by Donna Ogle and Camille Blachowicz

THE GUILFORD PRESS
New York   London

© 2008 The Guilford Press
A Division of Guilford Publications, Inc.
72 Spring Street, New York, NY 10012
www.guilford.com

All rights reserved

Except as indicated, no part of this book may be reproduced, translated,
stored in a retrieval system, or transmitted, in any form or by any means,
electronic, mechanical, photocopying, microfilming, recording, or otherwise,
without written permission from the Publisher.

Printed in the United States of America

This book is printed on acid-free paper.

Last digit is print number: 9   8   7   6   5   4   3   2   1

LIMITED PHOTOCOPY LICENSE

These materials are intended for use only by qualified professionals.

The Publisher grants to individual purchasers of this book nonassignable
permission to reproduce all materials for which photocopying permission
is specifically granted in a footnote. This license is limited to you, the
individual purchaser only, for use with your own clients or students.
Purchase by an institution does not constitute a site license. This license
does not grant the right to reproduce these materials for resale,
redistribution, or any other purposes (including but not limited to books
and handouts or slides for lectures or workshops). Permission to reproduce
these materials for these and any other purposes must be obtained in
writing from The Guilford Press.

Library of Congress Cataloging-in-Publication Data

Johnson, Denise.
    Teaching literacy in fourth grade / by Denise Johnson.
        p. cm. — (Tools for teaching literacy)
    Includes bibliographical references and index.
    ISBN-13: 978-1-59385-751-6 (pbk. : acid-free paper)
    ISBN-13: 978-1-59385-752-3 (hardcover : acid-free paper)
    1. Language arts (Primary)   2. Primary school teaching   3. Fourth grade
(Education)   I. Title.
    LB1576.J5914 2008
    372.6—dc22

                                                                2008007123

ABOUT THE AUTHOR

Denise Johnson, EdD, is Associate Professor of Reading Education at the College of William and Mary in Williamsburg, Virginia. She has worked as an elementary classroom teacher, a middle school reading specialist, and a Reading Recovery teacher. Her research interests include literacy, children's literature, and the integration of technology into literacy instruction.

SERIES EDITORS' NOTE

As teacher educators and staff developers we have become aware of the need for a series of books for thoughtful practitioners who want a practical, research-based introduction to teaching literacy at specific grade levels. Preservice and beginning teachers want to know how to be as effective as possible; they also know there are great differences in what students need across the grades. We have met teacher after teacher who, when starting to teach or moving to a new grade, asked for a guide targeted at their specific grade levels. Until now we didn't have a resource to share with them.

We also collaborate with staff developers and study group directors who want effective inservice materials that they can use with teachers at many different levels yet that still provide specific insights for individual grade levels. Thus the Tools for Teaching Literacy series was created.

This series is distinguished by two innovative characteristics designed to make it useful to individual teachers, staff developers, and study groups alike. Each Tools for Teaching Literacy volume:

➤ Is written by outstanding educators who are noted for their knowledge of research, theory, and best practices; who spend time in real classrooms working with teachers; and who are experienced staff developers who work alongside teachers applying these insights in classrooms. We think the series authors are unparalleled in these qualifications.

➤ Is organized according to a structure shared by all the grade-level books, which include chapters on:

- the nature of the learner at the particular grade level
- appropriate goals for literacy
- setting up the physical environment for literacy
- getting to know students with appropriate assessments and planning for differentiation

■ a week in the grade-level classroom—what this looks like in practice with important instructional strategies and routines

■ resources for learning

With this common organization in the grade-level books, a staff developer can use several different volumes in the series for teacher study groups, new teacher seminars, and other induction activities, choosing particular discussion and learning topics, such as classroom organization, that cross grade-level concerns. Teachers can also easily access information on topics of most importance to them and make comparisons across the grade levels.

In this volume, Denise Johnson introduces us to Julie Lipscomb and her fourth-grade class. Julie's focus on integrated instruction using informational text along with sample mini-lessons and examples of student work demonstrates what can be done to deepen literacy learning at this important transitional grade. The vivid descriptions and Julie's "voice" take us directly into the classroom and provide an exciting roadmap for new and developing teachers.

DONNA OGLE
CAMILLE BLACHOWICZ

CONTENTS

CHAPTER 1

WHAT IS THE FOURTH-GRADE CHILD LIKE?

> I ran to my room and slammed the door. . . . "My mother's the meanest mother in the whole world!" I told my turtle. "She loves Fudge more than me. She doesn't even love me anymore. She doesn't even like me. Maybe I'm not her real son. Maybe somebody left me in a basket on her doorstep. My real mother's probably a beautiful princess. I'll bet she'd like to have me back. Nobody needs me around here . . . that's for sure!"

Nine-year-old Peter Hatcher from Judy Blume's (1972, p. 38) *Tales of a Fourth Grade Nothing* captures the typical frame of mind of fourth graders. In the scene above, Peter's mother blamed him for his infamous 3-year-old brother, Fudge's, accident. Peter's exaggerated, irrational reaction is characteristic of many children during this preadolescent age. Later, when Peter's mom comes to his room and apologizes for unfairly blaming him for Fudge's accident, Peter is quickly appeased and thinks, "I knew she was my real mother after all." This "split personality" is a distinguishing factor of children in the "in between" or "tween" stage of life and typifies the 21 million children between the ages of 8 and 12. "The tween—too old to be a 'kid,' too young to be a teen. Too old to want to be totally dependent on parents; too young to have a work permit. To old to want to be associated with young kids; too young to be allowed into a PG-13 movie" (Siegel, Coffey, & Livingston, 2001, p. x).

This chapter highlights important influences and characteristics of the fourth-grade learner. Fourth-grade teachers such as Julie Lipscomb, whose teaching is discussed throughout this book, use their knowledge about children to guide and plan for instruction that accommodates all students' literacy needs and moves them toward becoming lifelong learners. When asked to describe the average fourth grader, Julie reflects:

> "I would describe a typical fourth grader as someone who comes to school ready to learn and expects school to be fun. Fourth graders have had previous

experiences and come with expectations. They still want to please, and most take suggestions readily. They are easy to bond with and quick to get to know."

This preadolescent period is a time of phenomenal cognitive, social, and emotional growth that is truly extraordinary.

INFLUENCES ON TODAY'S TWEENS

Though *Tales of a Fourth Grade Nothing* was written in 1972, Peter Hatcher is typical of today's fourth grader, physiologically and psychologically. Yet, we often hear parents, teachers, or other adults lament that today's tweens are different from when *they* (the adults) were kids. The difference between adults and today's tweens is their experiences. Parents of tweens are Generation X'ers who were children during a time of recession, huge national debt, downsizing, layoffs, and the emergence of HIV/AIDS. The experiences of today's 9- and 10-year-olds encompass Columbine, hanging chads, Osama bin Laden, 9/11, national security, al Qaeda, "axis of evil," Saddam Hussein, war in Iraq, insurgency, nuclear arms, global warming, Indian Ocean tsunami, Hurricane Katrina, Pakistan earthquake, No Child Left Behind, Harry Potter, the Internet, and widespread divorce. The old adage "experience is the best teacher" is true; these events certainly influence the way children interpret the world. As children encounter new experiences, existing memory structures in the brain, or schemas, are reshaped, impacting the linguistic, cognitive, social, and emotional development of children over time. Therefore, learning is not the *result* of development; learning *is* development. For example, as a result of their childhood experiences, Generation X'ers typically value good jobs and a good life, and they do everything they can to give their children what they want when they want it. Only time will tell what influence parents' actions and childhood events will have on today's tweens, but some logical conclusions might involve the desire for instant gratification, the motivation to achieve and succeed, conservative political beliefs that support expected future wealth, and social values that reflect environmental consciousness, global peace, and an understanding of diverse family structures.

Consumer marketing has quickly picked up on the economic force of the tween segment of the population. According to *BusinessWeek* (2007), 21 million tweens control more than $50 billion in purchasing power. Today's fourth graders have grown up with fast food, fashion, movies, television programming, cell phones, magazines and books, music, technology, and video games created and marketed just for them. Tweens have a great deal of leisure time they spend actively engaged with the latest technology, downloading music to their i-Pods and cell phones, updating their blogs, and playing games on the Internet. Tweens often have their own bedrooms, which have been decorated with items they selected. Book and magazine choices are directly related to their lifestyle interests.

It is important for fourth-grade teachers to understand the influences on 9- and 10-year-olds' lifestyles in order to provide a supportive environment and developmentally appropriate literacy instruction. For example, Julie's knowledge of her students' lives inside and outside the classroom helps her create a community of learners. Julie notes:

> "Our community of fourth graders helps everyone who is part of it. We learn everyone's strengths and weaknesses, which helps us see our differences and similarities. We listen to and respect each other's ideas and thoughts. I give students time to explain and let them ask questions and always share as a group. The openness allows them to feel they are a part of the community and that I respect them and their thoughts and ideas. I also try to find out about them personally and use that knowledge in my lessons to appeal to each of them. Of course, we all have to laugh as part of our day, and I laugh at myself when I make mistakes too."

Exemplary fourth-grade teachers understand that a child's potential for learning is revealed by, and even realized through, interactions with more knowledgeable others. These teachers are experts at keeping students engaged with learning by making connections to their personal interests and real world activities (Block & Mangieri, 2003). In addition to parental and consumer influences, an understanding of cognitive, social, emotional, and developmental influences provides significant implications for the construction of appropriate literacy instruction for children.

WHAT WE KNOW ABOUT THE DEVELOPMENT OF 9- AND 10-YEAR-OLDS

Literacy learning for children is necessarily interconnected with the nature of their development. The tween years are a time of major transitions cognitively, socially, and emotionally. Research in past decades by cognitive psychologists, most notably Swiss psychologist Jean Piaget, has informed our view of how children develop and learn. Though children progress at different rates, fourth graders are typically in the concrete operations stage of Piaget's stages of cognitive development. In this stage a child has the cognitive ability to use logical thought and perception to solve concrete problems. The power of logic and comprehension increases the child's ability to understand and appreciate more complex storylines and sophisticated humor.

Socially, children become less egocentric, a perspective that fosters an increasing importance of peers and an understanding of divergent perspectives. Friendship no longer means just someone to play with; now a friend is someone on whom to count and with whom to do things. It becomes important to watch the same television programs and movies, participate in the same sports and hobbies, and like the same music and books. Children typically have not yet developed the ability to think in the abstract; they are still bound by their perceptions of what is right, correct, or logical—aptly exhibited by an "it's not fair" attitude. Nevertheless, many children are beginning to develop a sense of social justice and to think more about what is good for the whole.

Fourth graders are also experiencing emotional transitions. Hormonal changes may lead to fluctuating emotions. Some children may become easily frustrated or suddenly start to cry or complain angrily when dealing with stressful situations, whereas others remain calm. Yet, most 9- and 10-year-olds have not experienced the governing sense of self-consciousness that characterizes older teens and are generally very positive and energized.

Social, emotional, and cognitive development are complementary processes that ultimately work together to shape a child's literacy growth. Figure 1.1 is an acrostic poem written by Dominic, a fourth grader in Julie's class. Dominic's poem highlights his talents and the activities in his life. It is important to note that Dominic considers himself a reader.

Students entering the fourth grade typically have a varied range of literacy capabilities. Some students may have experienced difficulty with learning to read

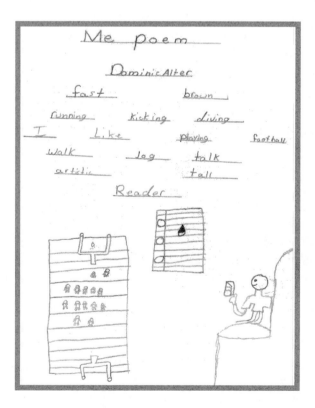

FIGURE 1.1. Dominic's acrostic "Me Poem."

and/or may be unmotivated to read, whereas others are avid readers and talk about books with peers. The following section describes the fourth-grade reader.

THE FOURTH-GRADE READER

"Probably the most difficult part of teaching fourth graders is the differences in abilities and what skills they bring with them. Some children struggle with reading and writing, and fourth grade is really a time to integrate reading with science and social studies. It can be challenging to find materials on some topics at lower reading levels with enough content to connect with student learning. Yet, these children want to read and enjoy learning just like the rest of the class."

As Julie shows in the above statement, fourth graders are in a period of transition in literacy development. The literacy experiences of students in the primary grades (K–3) focuses on learning to read with an emphasis on reading as a meaning-making process, understanding story patterns and language of narrative text, decoding and acquisition of sight vocabulary, development of word identification strategies, development of reading fluency, and the use of comprehension strategies for literal and inferential thinking. The content-area curriculum of many primary grades alternates the teaching of science and social studies every 6–9 weeks, and many do not use textbooks. Without this critical base, many kids are not equipped to do the abstract thinking and learning required of them as they move to the next grade. In fact, students who struggle with reading early in school often continue to struggle through the grades, especially with content-area texts (Francis, Shaywitz, Stuebing, Shaywitz, & Fletcher, 1996; Brozo & Simpson, 2007). Furthermore, children from low-income backgrounds and those with limited English skills are especially vulnerable to failure without appropriate instructional supports.

The scope and content of the typical fourth-grade curriculum can seem stark in comparison to the K–3 curriculum just described. All content areas are taught at scheduled times each day with required textbooks for each subject. Students must broaden their experience from reading primarily narrative texts to reading nonfiction, and they must develop both metacognitive strategies for coping with content material and study strategies. Students must comprehend increasingly complex reading material, enlarge their vocabulary, and build stamina for reading and writing for longer periods of time. Unfortunately, kids read less as they get older. According to a 2006 survey by Scholastic, 40% of kids between the ages of 5 and 8 read every day; by fourth grade, though, the rate had declined to 29%.

In addition to the increasing complexity of cognitive demands, fourth grade is typically the starting point for the national testing that is conducted across the United States. It is easy to see why the term "fourth grade slump" has been used to describe the challenges of teaching fourth grade, which is marked by a declining interest in reading and a gradual disengagement from school. The next section provides a broad overview of the fourth-grade reader, as based on the results of the National Assessment of Educational Progress (NAEP) and the Progress in International Reading Literacy Study (PIRLS).

Academic Achievement

The NAEP, commonly referred to as the "nation's report card," is a large-scale test that is given every few years in all states to measure students' knowledge of basic skills in various subjects in grades 4, 8, and 12. The reading assessment measures reading performance in two dimensions: reading contexts (reading for literary experience, reading for information, and reading to perform tasks) and aspects of reading (forming a general understanding, developing interpretation, making reader–text connections, and examining content and structure). Results of the assessment are reported on a 0–500 scale as well as achievement levels (basic, proficient, and advanced). The results of the reading assessment can give us a broad snapshot of what the nation's fourth graders are able to read and understand.

Overall scores from 1992 to 2005 on the NAEP reading assessment of fourth grade showed no significant gains (217 in 1992; 219 in 2005). However, overall scores from the 2007 administration showed a small but significant gain (217 in 1992; 221 in 2007). Gains were also made in two of the reading contexts: reading for literary experience and reading for information. In addition, performance increases were found in achievement levels: 67% of students are reading at the basic level, 33% at the proficient level, and 8% at the advanced level.

The NAEP also gives educators information on the achievement gap between racial/ethnic groups, socioeconomic groups, and males and females. White, black, Asian/Pacific Islander, and Hispanic fourth-grade students all scored higher in 2007 on the reading assessment than in the first assessment given 15 years ago. Unfortunately, improvements for minority students did not always narrow the achievement gaps with white students. Only the white–black gap at fourth grade was smaller in comparison to the gaps in 2005 and 1992. Students' eligibility for free or reduced-price lunch was used as an indicator of socioeconomic status. Students not eligible (higher-income families) scored higher than students who were eligible (lower-income families). Additionally, female students scored 7 points higher than male students, which is not significantly different from the gap seen 15 years ago. The overall picture indicates that although fourth-grade students' reading comprehension improved slightly in 2007 compared to the previous 13 years, a large majority (67%) comprehends at only a basic level. Contributing factors include the achievement gap that persists between racial/ethnic groups, socioeconomic groups, and gender. However, the NAEP does not provide information about factors that may be associated with the acquisition of reading, such as self-concept and attitude toward reading and literacy outside of school. For this information, we turn to the PIRLS, an assessment of reading comprehension conducted by the International Association for the Evaluation of Educational Achievement (IEA). The first study in a planned 5-year cycle of international trend studies was conducted in 2001. Thirty-five countries assessed the reading literacy of their 9-year-old students (fourth grade in most countries, including the United States). Both NAEP and PIRLS assess reading similarly; however, the PIRLS includes assessment of students' attitude toward reading and their literacy activities outside of school.

Reading Attitudes and Outside Influences

Results of the 2001 PIRLS assessment of reading attitude (see Table 1.1) were based on students' responses to the following questions:

➢ I read only if I have to. (reverse coded)

➢ I like talking about books with other people.

➢ I would be happy if someone gave me a book as a present.

➢ I think reading is boring. (reverse coded)

➢ I enjoy reading.

Students responded on a 4-point scale ranging from "disagree a lot" to "agree a lot." Students in the high category agreed or agreed a lot with all of the statements about reading, and students in the low category disagreed or disagreed a lot with all of the statements. The medium level indicates all other combinations of responses.

Students' attitudes toward reading were generally positive, with a little less than half categorized in the high category. However, a large discrepancy exists between girls' and boys' attitude toward reading in the high and low categories, with 19% more girls in the high category than boys, and 11% more boys in the low category than girls.

Results of the 2001 PIRLS assessment of reading self-concept (see Table 1.1) were based on students' responses to the following questions:

TABLE 1.1. 2001 PIRLS Results for Attitudes toward Reading

	Overall			Boys			Girls		
	H	M	L	H	M	L	H	M	L
Attitude toward reading	42	44	13	33	49	19	52	40	8
Reading self-concept	46	47	7	45	47	8	47	47	5

Note. H, high; M, medium; L, low.

➢ Reading is very easy for me.

➢ I do not read as well as other students in my class. (reverse coded)

➢ Reading aloud is very hard for me. (reverse coded)

Students' responses were categorized similarly to the reading attitude responses. Students' self-concept of their reading abilities and limitations were also generally positive, with almost half categorized in the high category. An important difference, however, is that boys' and girls' self-concepts of reading abilities and limitations were very similar, possibly indicating that though boys do not necessarily enjoy or appreciate books, they believe they are good readers.

The PIRLS also assessed the activities in which students engage outside of school. PIRLS asked:

➢ How often students read different types of text when they are not in school

➢ Frequency with which students read different types of text

➢ How often students read stories or novels outside of school

➢ How often students read for information outside of school (books that explain things, magazines, newspapers, and directions or instructions)

➢ How often students talked with their families about their reading

➢ How often students watched television or videos on a normal school day

The following results for U.S. fourth graders were gathered from the assessment:

➢ Thirty-five percent of students report reading for fun every day or almost every day; 22% report reading once or twice a week; 12% report reading once or twice a month; and 32% report reading never or almost never.

➢ Students who read for fun every day or almost every day have higher average scores on the combined reading literacy scale compared to those who never or almost never read for fun, or do so once or twice a month.

➢ Ninety-two percent of students report reading for information at least once or twice a month, a higher percentage than those who report reading either literary fiction, such as stories or novels (79%), or comics (43%) at least once or twice a month.

➢ Forty-three percent of students report that they read comics at least once or twice a month, a significantly lower percentage than the international average of 74%.

➢ Students who report reading literary fiction outside of school at least once or twice a month have higher scores on the combined reading literacy scale than those who never or almost never do so.

> ➢ No measurable differences in scores on the combined reading literacy scale are detected between students who read informational materials every day or almost every day, and those who never or almost never do so.

> ➢ Fifty-five percent of parents report that their child talks to them daily or once or twice a week about his or her reading.

> ➢ Eleven percent of students watch 3–5 hours of TV or videos on a normal school day, and 18% report watching TV or videos on a normal school day for 5 hours or more.

> ➢ Students who watch TV for more than 5 hours on a normal school day score lower than those who watch TV for 3–5 hours a day or less frequently.

One of the key findings from the results of this assessment is that almost half of fourth-grade students seldom or never read for fun outside of school, and those students did not score as well on the PIRLS reading assessment as students who read every day or once or twice a week. This result could be due to the fact that a significant portion of students (29%) watch 3 or more hours of TV or videos on a normal school day. These students may be choosing to watch TV or videos rather than reading for fun. Another important finding is that students engaged in more informational reading than fictional reading outside of school, indicating that, given a choice, many students will choose to read informational text over other genres.

This national perspective of fourth graders as readers inside and outside of school can provide teachers with some insight into their students' general reading achievement and activities outside of school that can contribute to their success or decline and disengagement in school. The "big picture" can help teachers focus on issues that might concern them about their own students as readers inside and outside of school. In the next section, we consider how Julie gathered information from her students at the beginning of the school year that informed her teaching throughout the year.

Julie's Students

Julie knows it is important to be aware of her students' reading strategies, attitudes, and outside influences in order to meet their needs and to motivate and engage them in meaningful reading and writing. To this end, she constructed a reading attitude/interest inventory and administered it to her students at the beginning of the school year. The results of the survey (see Table 1.2) will provide her with important information that she will use for initial and ongoing instructional decisions.

Much of the information Julie collected from her fourth graders is consistent with that of the national assessments discussed previously. A large majority of her students enjoy reading, read every day or every week, and consider themselves

TABLE 1.2. Reading Strategy Use, Attitude, and Outside Influences on Julie's Fourth-Grade Class

Question	Response	Yes	No	B	G
Do you like to read?	Those indicating they did not like to read stated it was because it was boring.	85%	15%	62%	100%
How often do you read?	55% every day; 20% once or twice a week; 25% seldom or never			77% every day	100% every day
What are your favorite types of books?	55% fantasy; 15% realistic fiction; 15% nonfiction; 8 % comics; 7% none				
What are some books you would like to own?	78% listed the title of a book they would like to own: 22% realistic fiction; 15% fantasy; 33% nonfiction; 7% comics; 22% did not list a book title			54% listed a title	100% listed a title
Do you have a favorite author?	Of those who listed an author only one was able to list the name—others only listed the title of the author's book(s).	30%	70%	15% listed a favorite author	29% listed a favorite author
Do you have a library card?	61% who had a library card used it once or more a month.	74%	26%	69%	100%
Do you read the newspaper?	The vast majority of students who read the newspaper listed comics as the section they most often read.	78%	22%	54%	86%
Do you read magazines?	Magazine titles ranged from *People* to *Sports Illustrated.*	70%	30%	46%	64%
Do you listen to audiobooks?		22%	78%	23%	21%
Do you like to be read to?	Reasons for *not* liking to be read to were: "Because I have trouble concentrating"; "It makes me sleepy"; "I'm too old; and "It makes me feel like a baby."	78%	22%	100%	71%
Do you recommend books to others?		59%	41%	54%	64%

Question	Response			
What do you think you do best in reading?	52%, "I don't know"; 19%, figure out words; 7%, read fast; 7%, imagine things well; 7%, read silently; 4%, "ask myself questions"; 4%, relax.			
What do you do when you have trouble reading a word?	55%, sound it out; 15%, ask someone for help; 11%, "I don't know"; 7%, say it slowly; 4%, "look for chunks I know"; 4%, use a dictionary; 4%, skip it.			
What do you do when you don't understand something you are reading?	37%, ask someone for help; 22%, reread the page; 15%, "I don't know"; 15%, choose another book; 7%, "read on to see if I understand"; 4%, use a dictionary.			
Do you think you are a good reader?	Of those who indicated they were not a good reader, the reason listed was because they were a slow reader.	85%	15%	100%
What do you think would be a good goal for you in reading this year?	Almost all students indicated that their goal was to be able to read longer/harder books or to learn new/harder words.			
Do you have a computer at home?	Commonly cited websites students accessed were almost entirely commercial and included *www.webkinz.com, www.spiderman.com,* and YouTube.	81%	19%	77%
Do you watch TV?	All students listed a variety of favorite television shows, which included cartoons and shows aimed at the tween audience.	100%		69%
Do you have a hobby?	Hobbies were varied and included sports, video games, and collecting various items (e.g., rocks, cards)	92%	8%	93%
Do you have a favorite movie?	All students listed one or more movies usually targeted at children/young adults (i.e., *Shrek III, Harry Potter V,* and *Spiderman III*).	100%		93%

Note. B, boys; G, girls.

good readers. A majority read the newspaper (mostly comics) and magazines. A large majority has a computer at home, watches television and movies, and has one or more hobbies. Julie also asked the students questions that allowed her to assess the type of books they like to read and their access to such books. Most students choose to read fantasy books and checked books out of the public library. However, when asked about a book they would like to own, most chose a nonfiction title. No student listed historical fiction as a genre he or she liked, has read, or would want to read. Most students didn't have a favorite author or listen to audio books. The majority of students liked to be read to and slightly more than half recommended books to others. Julie also asked questions that helped her assess the students' use of strategies and goals for reading. When asked about reading strategies for figuring out words or understanding the story, a majority of the students stated they did not know or listed strategies such as "ask someone for help." Overall, the information gained from the reading attitude/interest inventory lets Julie know that she will need to broaden her students' engagement with a variety of genres and tap into their interest in nonfiction and outside of school activities to reach those students who do not find reading enjoyable. She will build her students' awareness of the effective strategies they are using and teach them many more strategies for figuring out new vocabulary and understanding texts across genres and content-area reading and writing.

Also consistent with the national picture of fourth-grade readers is the discrepancy between the girls' and boys' reading attitudes and interests in Julie's class. The boys had a poorer attitude toward reading, spent less time reading, read fewer types of materials, and had fewer books they wanted to own. However, the boys did like to be read to more than the girls. Since reading aloud is a big part of Julie's instructional approach to literacy instruction, she will use read-alouds as a way to build interest and engagement with the boys in her class while simultaneously ensuring that the girls understand the importance of the read-aloud to literacy and learning. The RAND study of reading comprehension (2002) found that a child's self-concept of reading is critical to reading success:

> Still another important determinant of variability in reading comprehension is a reader's perceptions of how competent she or he is as a reader. For both younger and older students, it is the belief in oneself (or the lack thereof) that makes a difference in how competent they feel (Pajares, 1996). Providing students who are experiencing reading difficulties with clear goals for a comprehension task and then giving them feedback on the progress they are making can lead to increased self-efficacy and a greater use of comprehension (Dillon, 1989; Schunk & Rice, 1993). The degree to which these components develop in a younger or an older student may account, in part, for individual differences in the development of reading comprehension abilities. (p. 23)

Research has found that boys, in particular, are drawn to nonfiction (Brozo, 2002; Coles & Hall, 2001; Murphy & Elwood, 1998; Smith & Wilhelm, 2004; Taylor, 2005). Boys prefer texts that connect directly to their lives (their desires, concerns, experiences), that are appropriately challenging, and in which they can become totally immersed (Smith & Wilhelm, 2004). Such texts include informational books, magazines, and Internet sites that schools often don't recognize or embrace (Coles & Hall, 2001). Classroom libraries must reflect the interests of all children, and visually, intellectually, and emotionally appealing nonfiction of high quality should constitute a significant part of the collection. In this way, boys are given the chance to read books they find interesting, motivating, and engaging. In addition, boys must be exposed to a variety of genres and participate in school literacy practices. Educators must make efforts to provide structured opportunities for boys and girls to become emotionally engaged with text and to talk and write about the texts they are reading. Smith and Wilhelm (2004) suggest (1) "sequencing instruction so that success with one text or interpretive activity lays the groundwork for success in the next," and (2) "use think-aloud strategies and drama and visual art activities as supports to build on students' strengths in other semiotic systems so that they may be applied to more traditional forms of text" (p. 460). Julie will use the information she has gained from the survey to tailor instruction to her students' needs and to inform her selection of materials for the classroom library, her recommendations for reading to individual students, and her instructional materials.

As is discussed throughout the chapters in this book, excellent fourth-grade literacy teachers use instructional frameworks that vary instruction so that lessons move up or down the cognitive scale to adapt to students' needs and motivate them by keeping them engaged. The following section highlights instructional approaches that meet student needs (based on typical developmental characteristics of fourth graders).

Using Knowledge of Fourth Graders to Plan Literacy Learning

As emphasized in this chapter, teachers' knowledge of the influences and developmental characteristics of fourth graders is critical to creating a supportive learning community and to meeting the literacy needs of all children. Figure 1.2 provides an overview of the characteristics of the fourth-grade child with implications for teaching.

In the classroom, concurrent or follow-up discussions with the teacher and peers about a book read to, with, or by children may facilitate the course of cognitive development. Leading children to label, compare, explain, and classify new information or exposing children to other points of view and to conflicting ideas may encourage them to rethink or review their ideas. This type of interaction also promotes social development as children learn to value and appreciate the opinions of others. In addition, such discussions promote language development as the child is immersed in the conventions and pronunciations of language during literature response exchanges. These conversations must take place in a supportive environment in which the children feel safe and know that their responses will be respected.

Characteristics of child development for 9- to 10-year olds	Implications for literacy instruction
Cognitive development • Exhibits independence in reading, and a wide range of reading abilities and interests prevails • Concept of time and space continues to develop • Memory improves with increased attention span • Beginning to connect ideas and concepts as thoughts become flexible and reversible • Increasing capacity for problem solving, categorizing, and classifying *Language development* • Vocabulary continues to increase • Increased use of connectors such as *meanwhile, unless,* and *although* *Social and emotional development* • Influenced by social situations and peers • Sports and hobbies become more important • Searching for values; influenced by models other than family—those found in TV, movies, music, sports, books • Developing empathy for others as concepts of right and wrong become more flexible	• Read aloud more sophisticated fiction and nonfiction picture books and poetry every day • Read aloud longer chapter books with more variety, perspectives, and issues to promote interest and appreciation for a variety of genre • Provide sustained small-group and whole-class opportunities to respond to literature with peers and the teacher and through writing • Actively involve students in small-group and whole-class shared reading in which the teacher engages students in discussion, modeling, and demonstrations of more complex reading strategies that promote understanding of literary devices, vocabulary development, connections to text, and graphic aids in fiction and nonfiction texts • With guidance, provide opportunities for students to self-select a variety of fiction and nonfiction books, including series books, biographies, how-to books, riddles, comics, magazines, and online articles • Provide students with opportunities for storytelling and dramatization of stories, Readers' Theatre, and choral reading

FIGURE 1.2. Developmental characteristics of the fourth-grade child.

CHAPTER OVERVIEWS

The subsequent chapters in this book delve more deeply into the routines, planning, and instruction that support teaching and learning in fourth grade. Chapter 2 briefly summarizes the current political landscape of No Child Left Behind, which establishes accountability through standardized testing that is commonly conducted in fourth grade. The chapter also discusses what is known as "the fourth-grade slump." Together, these two challenges of teaching fourth grade can be formidable for educators. Resources such as *Standards for the English Language Arts* (IRA & NCTE, 1996) and research identifying the elements that contribute to students' success at meeting the standards can assist teachers in knowing what to teach in meaningful and motivating ways. The chapter concludes with insights from successful fourth-grade teachers.

Chapter 3 explores the whole-class, small-group, and individual instruction that must take place in order for teachers to meet the needs of all children in the classroom. This chapter examines organizational and instructional frameworks for achieving literacy goals and concludes with a look inside one teacher's fourth-grade classroom.

Chapter 4 addresses the need for initial and ongoing assessment to inform instruction in the fourth-grade classroom. Reading inventories and other methods of informing literacy instruction, ways to organize and analyze the plethora of assessment information, and the importance of conducting ongoing assessment to monitor students' learning and adjust instruction throughout the school year are discussed.

Chapter 5 focuses on the importance of making learning meaningful to all fourth graders, but specifically the importance of connecting learning to the experiences of struggling and at-risk students. Teachers' language of instruction and their use of just-right books are critical in helping children make sense of learning and play an essential role in scaffolding, modeling, and explicit instruction.

Chapter 6 brings together all of the components discussed in the previous chapters by highlighting a week in the inclusive classroom of veteran teacher Julie Lipscomb. Sometimes, "seeing is believing," so this chapter attempts to paint a picture of how Julie uses her knowledge of fourth graders and effective instructional practices to create a learning environment that meets the needs of all students in her classroom.

Research indicates that as children get older, parents start to become less involved in their school lives. It is important for teachers to maintain open communication with parents and find ways to bring them into the classroom community. Chapter 7 presents several ways to involve parents and keep them informed about what is going on in the classroom.

Finally, Chapter 8 includes a list of resources to support teachers in meeting the literacy needs of all children.

REFERENCES

Block, C. C., & Mangieri, J. N. (2003). *Exemplary literacy teachers: Promoting success for all children in grades K–5.* New York: Guilford Press.

Brozo, W. (2002). *To be a boy, to be a reader.* Newark, DE: International Reading Association.

Brozo, W., & Simpson, M. (2007). *Content literacy for today's adolescents: Honoring diversity and building competence.* Upper Saddle River, NJ: Merrill/Prentice Hall.

BusinessWeek. (2007, February 5). Tween power: Purchasing strength of kids. Available at *feedroom.businessweek.com*

Coles, M., & Hall, C. (2001). Boys, books and breaking boundaries: Developing literacy in and out of school. In W. Martino & B. Meyenn (Eds.), *What about the boys?: Issues of masculinity in schools* (pp. 211–221). Buckingham, UK: Open University Press.

Francis, D., Shaywitz, S., Stuebing, K., Shaywitz, B., & Fletcher, J. (1996). Developmental lag versus deficit models of reading disability: A longitudinal, individual growth curves analysis. *Journal of Educational Psychology, 88,* 3–17.

International Reading Association and the National Council of Teachers of English. (1996). *Standards for the English language arts.* Newark, DE: International Reading Association.

Martin, M., Mullis, I., & Kennedy, A. (Eds.). (2003). *Progress in international reading literacy study 2001 technical report.* Chestnut Hill, MA: Boston College.

Murphy, P., & Elwood, J. (1998). Gendered learning outside and inside school: Influences on achievement. In D. Epstein, J. Ellwood, V. Hey, & J. Maw (Eds.), *Failing boys: Issues in gender and achievement* (pp. 162–181). Buckingham, UK: Open University Press.

National Assessment of Educational Progress. (2007). *The Nation's Report Card: Reading 2007.* Washington, DC: Department of Education.

RAND Study Group. (2002). *Reading for understanding: Toward an R&D program in reading comprehension.* Arlington, VA: RAND Corporation.

Siegel, D., Coffey, T., & Livingston, G. (2001). *The great tween buying machine: Marketing to today's tween.* Ithaca, NY: Paramount Market.

Smith, M., & Wilhelm, J. (2004). "I just like being good at it": The importance of competence in the literate lives of young men. *Journal of Adolescent and Adult Literacy, 47*(6), 454–461.

Taylor, D. (2005). "Not just boring stories": Reconsidering the gender gap for boys. *Journal of Adolescent and Adult Literacy, 48*(6), 290–298.

Yankelovich and Scholastic. (2006, June). *Kids and family reading report.* New York: Scholastic. Available at *www.scholastic.com/aboutscholastic/news/readingreport.htm*

CHILDREN'S LITERATURE

Blume, J. (1972). *Tales of a fourth grade nothing.* New York: Dutton.

CHAPTER 2

KNOWING WHAT TO TEACH IN FOURTH GRADE

NO CHILD LEFT BEHIND AND STANDARDIZED TESTING IN FOURTH GRADE

Schools bring together children from diverse cultural, linguistic, and economic backgrounds. For some children entering fourth grade, the challenge of reading more widely and deeply in fiction and nonfiction subject-area textbooks is easy, and for others it is difficult. It is the needs of all children in the classroom community that influence the teaching and learning of literacy. Effective teaching of all children requires good teaching decisions regarding individuals, but especially for children who depend primarily on school for their literacy learning (Bandura, 1997). Reading achievement for children of poverty and those from urban minorities has continued to decline exponentially (Cooter, 2003; National Assessment of Educational Progress, 2000). Children who do not learn to read well early in school are more likely to fail later in school (Chall, Jacobs, & Baldwin, 1990; Fielding, Kerr, & Rosier, 1998).

Concern over the widening achievement gap for America's schoolchildren has resulted in an unprecedented national focus on ways to improve reading instruction. The No Child Left Behind (NCLB) Act was designed to ensure that all children are able to read fluently by third grade and to help close the gap in literacy achievement between the rich and the poor. Under NCLB, the federal government mandated a single test-based accountability system for all states, annual testing, and disaggregation of test scores by students' racial and socioeconomic backgrounds. Schools must demonstrate adequate yearly progress in order to remain accredited. Some states have restricted the curriculum and teaching materials to emphasize only those subjects on the state mandated test and require students who do not pass to be retained until they do pass. This annual testing takes place in the fourth grade more than any other grade in the United States (National Center for Education Statistics, 2005). Consider these statistics:

➢ 43 states (86%) conduct minimum-competency testing in fourth grade, followed by fifth grade in 37 states (74%) and third grade in 35 states (70%).

➢ For 13 of the 43 states, fourth grade is the first year students take a minimum-competency test.

➢ 32 of the 43 states use scores from minimum-competency testing for placement or promotion decisions.

➢ 21 of the 43 states conduct minimum-competency testing in science and social studies in addition to reading and math (National Center for Education Statistics, 2004).

In addition to state mandated testing, the National Assessment of Educational Progress (NAEP), a large-scale test given every few years that measures students' knowledge of basic skills, commonly referred to as the Nation's Report Card, is given in fourth grade and also eighth and twelfth grades.

It is fair to say that if a teacher is assigned to fourth grade, he or she will more than likely be responsible for administering a state-mandated test. This responsibility may seem troubling since often teachers feel pressure for their students to perform well. This pressure comes from administrators and/or from the media attention given to the public ranking of schools based on the results of fourth-grade assessments. It is common for schools or school districts to mandate teachers' use of one-size-fits-all materials and test preparation activities to ensure student success. Yet, Allington, Johnston, and Day's (2002) research in expert fourth-grade teachers' classrooms found that "good fourth-grade teaching is an expert activity that is not amenable to any one-size-fits-all plan for instruction" (p. 462). Excellent fourth-grade teaching is a complex activity that does not rely on scripted materials standardized lessons, or test preparation materials. Rather, "these teachers believed that good instruction would lead to enhanced test performance. . . . It was the less effective teachers' classrooms that we found test preparation activity" (p. 746).

Julie teaches in a suburban school in Virginia where students in fourth grade are tested in reading, writing, math, and social studies. Julie's school has approximately 600 K–5 students, of which 80% is white, 14% black, 3% Hispanic, 2% Native American, and 1% Asian. Sixteen percent of the student population is economically disadvantaged, 12% has disabilities, and less than 1% is comprised of English language learners. The school achieved annual yearly progress in 2006. Recently, the school district instituted benchmark testing that is administered every 9 weeks from the beginning of the school year until the state-mandated test is given in May. Benchmark testing is intended to provide test-taking practice for students and to provide teachers and administrators with information as to how well children are doing at the time on the information they will be tested on later in the year. The benchmark tests take 3 days every 9 weeks away from instructional time. Although Julie does review content and strategies prior to taking the test, she devotes most of her time to regular classroom instruction. Julie states:

> "Although there is reviewing before the actual testing, much of reading and writing workshop is spent developing and nurturing the love of reading. The more the students read, the more exposure they will gain to vocabulary and analyzing literature of all kinds. They don't even realize they are preparing for the test because it is just part of talking about the books they love."

Teachers and administrators are not the only ones who feel the pressure from high-stakes testing. Children are affected as well. Some put pressure on themselves to do well, whereas others are pressured by parents and teachers. This level of pressure can be especially difficult if fourth grade is the first year in which students are tested. For example, as each testing period drew closer, one of Julie's students started to have stomachaches quite often. Julie did not think this child would be worried about testing, but as she continued to observe her, it became clear that she was nervous about the test. Julie decided to talk to the child: "I talked to her about my confidence in her abilities as a student and gave her examples of her success in the classroom, pointed out how she made herself successful. I also underscored the fact that her past test scores had been fine. I really wanted her to see that she had control over the situation." Outstanding fourth-grade teachers are very approachable and encourage students to focus on their talents, not on upcoming mandated tests.

The Fourth-Grade Slump and Nonfiction/Content-Area Reading

The "fourth-grade slump" is a term used to describe a decline in progress between the scores of fourth graders on national assessments and younger children (Snow, Burns, & Griffin, 1998). One explanation for this drop in achievement is the lack of attention given to comprehension in the primary grades. Students master basic reading skills but are challenged by the more complex tasks required of subject-area texts introduced in fourth grade.

Duke's (2000) research in 20 first-grade classrooms (10 in low-SES [socioeconomic status] districts and 10 in high-SES districts) found little time during the school day devoted to information text—a mean of 3.6% minutes per day. Additionally, classrooms in low-SES districts had less informational text and spent less time in activities using them—just 1.4 minutes per day. Duke argued that the lack of exposure to informational texts in first-grade classrooms in general, and low-SES classrooms in particular, may help explain why many children have difficulty with informational reading and writing later in school.

Content-area textbooks consist of nonfiction expository text written to inform or explain. Characteristics and conventions of expository text are significantly different from narrative text, which is read for aesthetic reasons and is typically more familiar to students because it predominates in the primary grades. Students employ their knowledge of linear story structure, story elements, and background knowledge to actively engage with the story. For example, if the story starts with "Once upon a time," then the reader's knowledge of the fairytale story structure instantly sets up a series of predictable story elements such as setting (castles), time period (long ago), characters (a princess, a witch), plot/events (the evil character will try to do something bad to the good character but will be foiled in the end), and resolution (the good characters live happily ever after).

Expository text is read to learn more about a subject. Instead of following a typical story structure, expository text uses an organization that makes sense for the content such as setting up cause-and-effect relationships, sequence or chronological order, description, and problem–solution or comparison–contrast structures. The reader might not read the whole book but use the table of contents or

TABLE 2.1. Comparisons of Narrative and Expository Text

Narrative	Expository
Follows a familiar story structure—characters, plot, theme, and setting—in the order of events	Organized by cause-and-effect connections, sequence, description, problem–solution, and comparison–contrast
Reader reads for aesthetic purposes (e.g., enjoyment, intrigue)	Reader reads to find out information
Illustrations extend text meaning	Illustrations (usually with captions) are used to clarify or explain
Written in past tense	Written in present tense
Uses prose paragraph style	Uses headings, subheadings, titles, table of contents, indexes, and glossaries
Uses dialogue and familiar vocabulary	Does not use dialogue; uses technical vocabulary
Concepts are usually related to the experiences of the reader	Subject may be about abstract concepts unfamiliar to the reader
Reader gets meaning from events and characters	Reader gets meaning from information
Reader suspends disbelief	Reader assumes information is accurate
Plots holds reader's attention	Reader attends to organization of information
Reader may read material quickly	Reader uses flexible, slower reading rate

index to find a particular part of the book that includes the desired information (see Table 2.1 for comparisons of narrative and expository text).

Duke's (2000) research supports the theory behind the fourth-grade slump in that lack of exposure to nonfiction at an early age has lasting effects into intermediate, middle, and high school for the obvious reason that children who are not provided with instruction on how to read nonfiction texts early in school will not have the necessary strategies for the content-area reading that predominates later in school. Therefore, fourth-grade teachers must skillfully and effectively teach students of varying literacy abilities how to (1) extract information from a textbook, (2) apply comprehension strategies in science and social studies, and (3) employ high levels of critical thinking. Block and Mangieri (2003) found that excellent fourth-grade teachers are able to achieve this goal through "coaching":

> The most distinguishing quality of excellent fourth-grade teachers in their role as Coaches, is their ability to instruct numerous students of diverse literacy abilities simultaneously during the same lesson. They achieve these objectives by giving assignments that have differentiated goals, by providing a wide range of books that can be read by students, and by varying the amounts of time required for the students to complete their various literacy lessons. In other words, they coach students to assume the primary responsibility for their own learning, yet these teachers continuously challenge and instruct students to increase their reading powers. (pp. 46–47)

Block and Mangieri's (2003) research found that the most important contribution to an exemplary fourth-grade teacher's literacy success is his or her ability to move each individual student's learning forward. For example, when Julie begins a unit in social studies on the Revolutionary War, she provides a variety of historical fiction books that ranges in difficulty to meet all students' reading levels. As they begin to read, Julie conferences with students individually to assess comprehension and provide individual strategy instruction. She may meet with some students longer or more often than others, depending on their needs. As they respond to the reading in their journals, she may ask students to explore certain aspects of their reading more fully. In this way, Julie coaches students with diverse literacy abilities, providing each with texts he or she can read and instruction that meets his or her individual needs to move forward in literacy learning.

So far in this chapter, two major instructional characteristics of exemplary fourth-grade teaching have been discussed: (1) Excellent fourth-grade teaching is a complex activity that does not rely on scripted materials, standardized lessons, or test preparation materials; and (2) excellent fourth-grade teaching provides differentiated instruction that moves each individual student's learning forward. If exemplary fourth-grade teachers do not use scripted materials and lessons and vary instruction to meet individual student's needs, the question remains: How do fourth-grade teachers know *which* strategies to teach?

STANDARDS FOR THE ENGLISH LANGUAGE ARTS

The *Standards for the English Language Arts*, developed by the International Reading Association (IRA) and the National Council of Teachers of English (1996), provide guidelines for assessment and instruction based on current research and theory about how students learn. The standards, listed in Figure 2.1, constitute a broad framework that can assist teachers in planning for instruction as they guide children on their journey toward becoming good readers. Often the national standards serve as a guideline for state and local school districts in developing specific standards or benchmarks at each grade level.

According to the ELA national standards, literacy instruction should produce competency in speaking, listening, reading, writing, viewing, and visually representing through nonverbal means. These six language systems are interrelated and should be taught together, rather than as separate lessons. Figure 2.2 shows how the various language arts support one another. Research has shown that exemplary teachers integrate language learning with the language arts, content-area learning, and literature study (Allington & Johnston, 2002; Pressley, Allington, Wharton-MacDonald, Collins-Block, & Morrow, 2001; Wharton-MacDonald, Pressley, & Hampston, 1998).

The IRA/NCTE standards are intended to provide long-term goals regarding what students should know and be able to do, but they are not designed in a way that helps teachers plan for daily instruction. For this, we turn to the *Performance Standards for Elementary School* (National Center on Education and the Economy, 2001). The elementary standards for ELA, math, science, and applied learning were developed in concert with the content standards produced by the national professional organizations for the disciplines. The standards for ELA were developed in concert with IRA/NCTE and are designed to take the next step in specifying "how good is good enough" (p. 3). The ELA performance standards consist of five domains: reading, writing, speaking/listening/viewing, conventions/grammar/usage, and literature. To gain insight into how the performance standards clearly identify what students should know and be able to do for each domain, the first performance standard for reading is presented in Figure 2.3.

With these standards as a guide, a fourth-grade teacher could discern the particular achievements expected within the reading domain. The next section examines the elements that contribute to students' success at meeting these standards.

ELEMENTS THAT CONTRIBUTE TO STUDENTS' SUCCESS AT MEETING STANDARDS

In order for students to achieve high levels of literacy learning, teachers must create nurturing environments that support the development of good readers. A

The vision guiding these standards is that all students must have the opportunities and resources to develop the language skills they need to pursue life's goals and to participate fully as informed, productive members of society. These standards assume that literacy growth begins before children enter school as they experience and experiment with literacy activities—reading and writing, and associating spoken words with their graphic representations. Recognizing this fact, these standards encourage the development of curriculum and instruction that make productive use of the emerging literacy abilities that children bring to school. Furthermore, the standards provide ample room for the innovation and creativity essential to teaching and learning. They are not prescriptions for particular curriculum or instruction. Although we present these standards as a list, we want to emphasize that they are not distinct and separable; they are, in fact, interrelated and should be considered as a whole.

1. Students read a wide range of print and non-print texts to build an understanding of texts, of themselves, and of the cultures of the United States and the world; to acquire new information; to respond to the needs and demands of society and the workplace; and for personal fulfillment. Among these texts are fiction and nonfiction, classic and contemporary works.	2. Students conduct research on issues and interests by generating ideas and questions, and by posing problems. They gather, evaluate, and synthesize data from a variety of sources (e.g., print and non-print texts, artifacts, people) to communicate their discoveries in ways that suit their purpose and audience.
3. Students read a wide range of literature from many periods and many genres to build an understanding of the many dimensions (e.g., philosophical, ethical, aesthetic) of human experience.	4. Students use a variety of technological and information resources (e.g., libraries, databases, computer networks, video) to gather and synthesize information and to create and communicate knowledge.
5. Students apply a wide range of strategies to comprehend, interpret, evaluate, and appreciate texts. They draw on their prior experience, their interactions with other readers and writers, their knowledge of word meaning and of other texts, their word identification strategies, and their understanding of textual features (e.g., sound–letter correspondence, sentence structure, context, graphics).	6. Students develop an understanding of and respect for diversity in language use, patterns, and dialects across cultures, ethnic groups, geographic regions, and social roles.
7. Students adjust their use of spoken, written, and visual language (e.g., conventions, style, vocabulary) to communicate effectively with a variety of audiences and for different purposes.	8. Students whose first language is not English make use of their first language to develop competency in the English language arts and to develop understanding of content across the curriculum.
9. Students employ a wide range of strategies as they write and use different writing process elements appropriately to communicate with different audiences for a variety of purposes.	10. Students participate as knowledgeable, reflective, creative, and critical members of a variety of literacy communities.
11. Students apply knowledge of language structure, language conventions (e.g., spelling and punctuation), media techniques, figurative language, and genre to create, critique, and discuss print and non-print texts.	12. Students use spoken, written, and visual language to accomplish their own purposes (e.g., for learning enjoyment, persuasion, and the exchange of information).

FIGURE 2.1. Standards for English Language Arts. From the International Reading Association and the National Council of Teachers of English (1996). Copyright 1996 by the International Reading Association and the National Council of Teachers of English. Reprinted by permission.

	Written language	Spoken communication	Visual literacy
Receptive language process	**Reading**	**Listening**	**Viewing**
	A cognitive process whereby individuals engage with written text, decode it and gain meaning from it.	Listening requires us to receive and make sense of the oral language of others.	Viewing and interpreting pictures, signs, commercial logos, computer graphics, TV, movies, video, and websites
Expressive language process	**Writing**	**Speaking**	**Visually representing**
	The reciprocal of reading, writing requires us to encode and produce written language.	When we talk we produce language. Speaking is the reciprocal of listening.	Making meaning from visual information conveyed through images such as art, Web pages, movies, drawings, and paintings

FIGURE 2.2. Integrated language arts. From Johnson (2008). Copyright 2008 by Houghton Mifflin. Reprinted by permission.

review of the research reveals several features of classroom contexts that support the development of good readers: (1) time to read self-selected texts, (2) access to varied and authentic texts, (3) explicit instruction in comprehension strategies, (4) explicit teaching of vocabulary and concept development, (5) the challenge of complex tasks, and (6) talk about texts (Allington, 2002; Duke & Pearson, 2002; Purcell-Gates, Duke, & Martineau, 2007; RAND Study Group, 2002). Each of these features is discussed in the following sections.

Time to Read Self-Selected Texts

Early in the spring, when the ground is still cold, gardeners till, weed, fertilize, and plant the seeds that will become beautiful plants and flowers later in the summer. Plants must be given time to germinate—to grow and develop. Likewise, providing time to read allows students the opportunity to orchestrate the skills and strategies that are important to skillful reading and to acquire new knowledge. Ample time for reading is defined as "more time to read than the combined total allocated for *learning* about reading and *talking* or *writing* about what has been read" (Fielding & Pearson, 1994, p. 63). Routman (2003) suggests that teachers keep in mind the 20%-to-80% rule wherein approximately one-fifth of the time allocated for reading each day is dedicated to explicit strategy instruction and in the remaining time students apply that instruction during actual reading.

Students should also be given the chance to choose their own books, reread texts for fluency, and read and discuss books with peers. Even with a teacher's caring guidance or a parent's well-intended recommendation of a book, children are more likely to turn to books that reflect *their* interests and preferences. It is the kind of reading highly literate people do all the time! When real-world readers

Performance Standard 1: Reading

The student reads at least twenty-five books or book equivalents each year. The materials should include traditional and contemporary literature (both fiction and nonfiction) as well as magazines, newspapers, textbooks, and online materials. Such reading should represent a diverse collection of material from at least three different literary forms and from at least five different writers.

Examples of activities through which students might produce evidence of reading twenty-five books include:
- Maintain an annotated list of works read.
- Generate a reading log or journal.
- Participate in formal and informal book talks.

The student reads and comprehends at least four books (or book equivalents) about one issue or subject, or four books by a singe writer, or four books in one genre, and produces evidence of reading that:
- makes and supports warranted and responsible assertions about the texts;
- supports assertions with elaborated and convincing evidence;
- draws the texts together to compare and contrast themes, characters, and ideas;
- makes perceptive and well developed connections;
- evaluates writing strategies and elements of the author's craft.

Examples of activities through which students might produce evidence of reading comprehension include:
- Make connections between literary works according to a common theme.
- Produce an informative report.
- Produce a literary response paper.
- Participate in formal or informal book talks.
- Create an annotated book list organized according to author, theme, or genre.

The student reads and comprehends informational materials to develop understanding and expertise and produces written or oral work that:
- restates or summarizes information;
- relates new information to prior knowledge and experiences;
- extends ideas;
- makes connections to related topics or information.

Examples of activities through which students might produce evidence of informational materials include:
- Contribute to an attribute book.
- Present information to an audience of peers.
- Produce a chapter book on a factual topic.
- Rewrite videogame instructions for a younger reader.

The student reads aloud, accurately (in the range of 85–90%), familiar material of the quality and complexity illustrated in the sample reading list, and in a way that makes meaning clear to listeners by:
- self correcting when subsequent reading indicates an earlier miscue;
- using a range of cueing systems, e.g., phonics and context clues, to determine pronunciation and meanings;
- reading with a rhythm, flow, and meter that sounds like everyday speech.

Examples of activities through which students might produce evidence of reading aloud accurately include:
- Read aloud to peers or younger children.
- Participate in Readers' Theatre production.
- Record on an audiotape or videotape an example of reading aloud.

FIGURE 2.3. Performance Standard 1: Reading. From National Center on Education and the Economy and the University of Pittsburgh (2001, p. 22). Copyright 2001 by the National Center on Education and the Economy and the University of Pittsburgh. Reprinted by permission.

choose a text, they are reading to learn and to enjoy. They accomplish these tasks by selecting a text that fulfills their needs. When given the chance, children will make positive selections based on both interest and ability. Research suggests that students can, and do, make choices that increase their awareness and extend their growing knowledge of literacy (Fresch, 1995; McLaughlin & Allen, 2002; Schlager, 1978; Worthy, 1996).

Access to Varied and Authentic Texts

The first performance standard for ELA listed previously is for students to read 25 quality books. A list of possible books is included as part of the standard. This list included such titles as *Caddie Woodlawn* (Brink, 1973), *Dinosaurs of North America* (Sattler, 1981), *Ego-Tripping and Other Poems for Young People* (Giovanni, 1973), *Legend of the Milky Way* (Lee, 1982), *The Lion, the Witch and the Wardrobe* (Lewis, 1960), and the magazine *Time for Kids*. These books and magazines are all authentic texts or trade books that you find in a library or book store, not specially constructed materials such as basals or anthologies and content-area textbooks. The Performance Standards state: "Too often students are not given the opportunity to read full-length books because of curricular restraints, a lack of resources, or a lack of access to books. The missed opportunity results in a tremendous loss of potential literacy skills that can only be developed when students become habitual readers" (p. 20). Not to be misunderstood, textbooks are a useful and necessary resource for the classroom. They provide the content set by the district curriculum and state and national standards, and they serve as a resource to the classroom teacher. But textbooks are limited in depth and perspective. Furthermore, teacher editions of content textbooks do not help students become strategic readers (Kragler, Walker, & Martin, 2005). Trade books generally

➢ Are more up-to-date.

➢ Contain less overwhelming vocabulary.

➢ Provide a more focused, in-depth look at particular subjects.

➢ Accommodate differences in learning styles.

➢ Have more interesting and less confusing storylines that help children remember concepts.

➢ Contain colorful pictures and graphics.

➢ Provide context for understanding difficult concepts.

➢ Have a more positive view of women and minorities.

Teachers can supplement textbooks with fiction and nonfiction trade books that can serve as a magnifying glass that enlarges and enhances the reader's personal interaction with a subject and provides motivation, enthusiasm, and insight

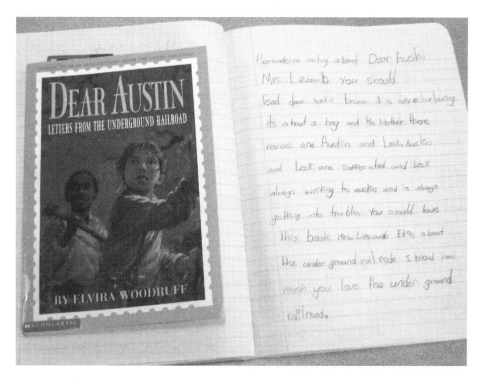

FIGURE 2.4. Authentic reading and writing integrated into the social studies curriculum.

into just about any aspect of the curriculum (see example in Figure 2.4). Including a range of authentic texts not only meets individual student interests and abilities, but also exposes students to other genres, topics, cultures, characters, minorities, and people with disabilities.

Experience reading real texts for real purposes will increase the likelihood that students will transfer the use of strategies to their independent reading. Most of us read a variety of nonfiction texts everyday—the newspaper, Internet articles, magazines, cookbooks, vacation brochures—because they present information of interest to us. "In contrast," Duke (2004) asserts, "students in school usually read informational text to answer questions at the back of the chapter, to complete a test prep worksheet, or simply because the teacher said so" (p. 42). Children must be given opportunities to read and write nonfiction texts for authentic reasons. In a recent study by Purcell-Gates and colleagues (2007), children in the second and third grades involved in authentic literacy events with informational and procedural texts in science showed an impressive degree of growth in their abilities to comprehend and write science texts.

The availability of quality nonfiction books has increased significantly in the past decade. Educators must ensure that a considerable portion of school and classroom libraries is devoted to nonfiction texts, among them concept books, picturebooks, photographic essays, Internet websites, journals and diaries, magazines, how-to books, field guides, newspaper articles, brochures, pamphlets, maps, and reference books. Not only does this array accommodate the interests, motivation, and engagement of students, but it sends a strong message that reading outside of school, which involves predominantly nonfiction texts, is also important inside of school.

Access to a critical mass of nonfiction books in the classroom is an important first step that then must be extended into opportunities for instruction.

Explicit Instruction in Comprehension Strategies

A review of the research on comprehension was conducted by the RAND Study Group, appointed by the U.S. Department of Education's Office of Educational Research and Improvement. The RAND Study Group (2002) defined reading comprehension, as "the process of simultaneously extracting and constructing meaning through interaction and involvement with written language" (p. 12). The RAND Study Group's review identified basic findings that research has established:

> Instruction can be effective in providing students with a repertoire of strategies that promote comprehension monitoring and foster comprehension.

> The explicitness with which teachers teach comprehension strategies makes a difference in learner outcomes, especially for low-achieving students.

> Teachers who provide comprehension strategy instruction that is deeply connected within the context of subject-matter learning, such as history and science, foster comprehension.

> Using various genres of text enhances students' knowledge of text structures, which is an important factor in fostering comprehension.

> Teachers who give students choices, challenging tasks, and collaborative learning structures increase students' motivation to read and comprehend text. (pp. 32–41)

With these points in mind, six comprehension strategies listed in Figure 2.5 have been found to be effective in improving children's comprehension of text.

Explicit strategy instruction has repeatedly been shown to have positive effects on comprehension, especially for poor comprehenders (Fielding & Pearson, 1994; RAND Study Group, 2002). Yet, the RAND Study Group (2002) found that typical classrooms across the primary and upper-elementary grades do not devote adequate time and attention to comprehension instruction. Duke and Pearson (2002) propose a gradual-release-of-responsibility model of comprehension instruction that includes the following five phases:

Comprehension strategy	Definition
Prediction/activating prior knowledge	Engaging students in making predictions about a story has been shown to increase interest and memory for stories, especially when the students' predictions are explicitly compared to text ideas during reading.
Thinking aloud	Thinking aloud is a way of making the invisible visible. When thinking aloud, during reading, the teacher or student verbalizes his or her thinking about how he or she went about accomplishing a strategy or skill. When a teacher thinks aloud, it can serve as a model of how to effectively employ a specific strategy.
Text structure	Understanding the underlying organizational structure of narrative and informational texts helps children relate ideas to one another in ways that make them more understandable and more memorable.
Visual representations of text	Involving students in constructing visual displays by using various visual tools such as semantic maps and webs has been shown to improve students' ability to organize what they are learning.
Summarization	Summarizing requires students to sift through large amounts of information, differentiate important from less important ideas, and then synthesize those ideas into a new text that contains the essential components of the original text. Summarization is a difficult task for many children and requires much instruction and practice.
Questions/questioning	In the area of improving students' comprehension, there is much research to support the need for teachers to ask students higher-level—inferential and evaluative—questions that require them to connect information in the text to their own knowledge base. Additionally, students must learn to ask questions themselves as they are reading.

FIGURE 2.5. Comprehension strategies. Based in part on Duke and Pearson (2002) and RAND Study Group (2002).

1. An explicit description of the strategy and when and how it should be used.
2. Teacher and/or student modeling of the strategy in action.
3. Collaborative use of the strategy in action.
4. Guided practice using the strategy with gradual release of responsibility.
5. Independent use of the strategy.

As one moves through the phases, students assume more responsibility and teachers less responsibility for task completion. In the beginning, the teacher is primarily responsible for performing the task, providing modeling, demonstrations, and guided practice. Then, as the teacher gradually releases responsibility, students begin to take over the task through guided participation and then independent performance. While students are participating in guided practice, the teacher facilitates and provides scaffolding when necessary. The gradual release of responsibility for a task may take place over a few days, weeks, or even months, depending on the task and students, and the release process should be flexible and dynamic. For example, after the teacher has modeled a task and then engages the students in guided practice, he or she may decide that more modeling is necessary.

When providing explicit instruction on comprehension strategies, it is important to assist students in understanding that readers do not use any one comprehension strategy in isolation of others. Good readers use multiple strategies simultaneously. For example, when a person starts to read a new book he or she will make predictions based on the cover, title, pictures, and information on the inside flap or back of the book. Based on this information, the reader will make connections to his or her background knowledge and understanding of the structure of the story, and then formulate questions about the plot or events. Making predictions, using background knowledge and text structure, and asking questions are all important comprehension strategies that assist the reader in comprehending the text. Though teachers may find it necessary to model and demonstrate a particular strategy at a particular time, other strategies should also be suggested, modeled, and integrated throughout the process (Dorn & Soffas, 2005; Duke & Pearson, 2002).

It is important to note that the RAND Study Group (2002) found that "accessing the Internet makes large demands on individuals' literacy skills; in some cases, this new technology requires readers to have novel literacy skills, and little is known about how to analyze or teach those skills" (p. 4). As indicated in Chapter 1, fourth graders are increasingly connected to the digital information highway. Digital texts and information and communications technology (ICTs) are quickly becoming the predominant way people read and communicate at work and home and will only become more pervasive. It is important for fourth-grade teachers to have an expanded definition of comprehension that includes understanding the genre of digital texts on the Internet and other ICTs, the new literacies required for reading, writing, and communicating in an increasingly digital world, and the potential for increased learning and motivation that are critical for effective instruction. Teachers can use these tools to extend children's understanding, motivation, and engagement with the curriculum in authentic ways that also extend opportunities to acquire the skills and strategies needed to live and work in the rapidly changing technological world.

Explicit Instruction in Vocabulary and Concept Development

Numerous studies have documented the salient role of vocabulary in reading comprehension and the fact that a child's vocabulary knowledge is highly predictive of her or his reading comprehension. Research has also shown that children from lower SES backgrounds have deficits in vocabulary knowledge compared to children from higher SES backgrounds, which contribute to the achievement gap (Beck, McKeown, & Kucan, 2002; Biemiller, 2001). These children, in particular, but all children, in general, need multiple daily opportunities to build vocabulary knowledge. Instruction in vocabulary involves far more than looking up words in a dictionary and using the words in a sentence. Rich and robust vocabulary instruction actively involves students in using and thinking about word meanings and in creating relationships among words. Vocabulary is acquired incidentally through indirect exposure to words, intentionally through explicit instruction in specialized and general-concept knowledge, and through independent word-learning strategies.

One of the most widely acknowledged ways of building students' vocabulary is incidentally through wide reading. Nagy (1988) states:

> Most growth in vocabulary knowledge must necessarily come though reading. There is no way that vocabulary instruction alone can provide students with enough experiences with enough words to produce both the depth and breadth of vocabulary knowledge that they need to attain. Increasing the volume of students' reading is the single most important thing a teacher can do to promote large-scale vocabulary growth. (p. 32)

Seeing vocabulary in rich contexts provided by authentic texts, rather than in isolated vocabulary drills, produces robust vocabulary learning. Good literature can take children to places that classroom experiences cannot, such as a visit to Hogwarts Academy in *Harry Potter*, a trip inside the human body on the *Magic School Bus*, or a microscopic view of insects in *Hidden Worlds: Looking through a Scientist's Microscope*. These vicarious experiences provide a powerful way to learn word meanings. Students can also learn word meanings incidentally from interactive read-aloud experiences, in which the teacher scaffolds learning by asking questions, adding information, or prompting students to describe their thinking before, during, and after listening to a book.

Fourth graders typically have a large sight/listening vocabulary and word identification strategies because these are the main emphases in the primary grades, but as students progress into more difficult material, they encounter words that are labels for concepts that can only be acquired through repeated exposure in a variety of meaningful contexts. Vocabulary development activities that focus on breaking words into syllables, looking for prefixes and suffixes or other word chunks, and using pronunciation keys will not help when words go beyond a student's experience, because these strategies do not help students deal with meanings of unfamiliar words. For example, a fourth grader who encounters the word *chlorophyll* in a science textbook may be able to use word identification strategies to figure out the pronunciation but will still not understand the meaning if it is not explicitly stated in the text or revealed through context clues. This type of specialized vocabulary goes beyond students' experiences.

With more general vocabulary, students might not know a word, but prior knowledge and experiences play an important part in their ability to use context clues for text comprehension. For example, a child might not know the word *infuriated* in the sentence, "The young woman was infuriated by the violence she saw on the television show." Yet, drawing on prior knowledge of how parents and teachers react to violence on television shows, the child would be able to approximate the meaning of the word. Specialized and general vocabulary learning requires direct instruction in order for students to acquire strategies for independent vocabulary acquisition. Figure 2.6 provides examples of vocabulary building activities that help students learn specific and general vocabulary.

In addition to teacher-directed vocabulary activities, students should be given strategies for learning words independently. One of the most useful strategies for figuring out unknown words is through context clues. As mentioned earlier, many times specialized vocabulary remains inaccessible to students, even if they try to use context clues, due to students' lack of prior knowledge or lack of context clues in the passage. Generally, however, context clues can be a very productive way to derive meaning from new words. Good readers tend to use context clues instinctively, whereas less strategic readers tend to isolate unknown words from relevant context. Teachers can demonstrate the process of using context clues. See the activities under "Approximate meanings" in Figure 2.6.

Vocabulary notebooks are also a way for students to become aware of new words encountered during independent reading. Students are encouraged to include three for four new words a week from a variety of genres. Figure 2.7 is a page from the vocabulary notebook of a student in Julie's fourth-grade class. An entire page is dedicated to each word. The word is written at the top of the page; in this example, the student has drawn a visual representation of the word *directionless*. Students could also include:

➢ The original sentence in which the word was found.

➢ Synonyms or other words associated with the new word.

➢ A new sentence created by the student using the word.

The purpose of a vocabulary notebook is to promote students' independent vocabulary knowledge and to provide multiple contexts in which students become familiar with the word. Since students are working independently, they might derive an incorrect meaning of the word. To ensure that they have the correct meaning, students can check with peers or the teacher.

The Challenge of Complex Tasks

Fourth graders are truly interested in many of the topics in the curriculum and, if given the chance, will engage in further reading and writing about these topics, both collaboratively and independently. Allington (2002) and Block and Mangieri's (2003) research found that an important characteristic of exemplary fourth-grade classrooms is teachers' engagement of students in longer-term literacy projects (than those assigned in the primary grades) integrated across the curriculum. Allington (2002) observed:

Activity	Description	Example
Approximate meanings	• Teacher provides a sentence using the word, and students approximate the definition from context. • Teacher dramatizes the words. • Students brainstorm experiences related to the word.	• The girl was *diffident* about her appearance and slouched as she walked. • The teacher provides an example of a dramatization of the word. For the word *diffident*, she might slouch, look around nervously, and avoid the attention of others. • The teacher asks students to relate any personal experiences they have had or situations that would make them feel diffident.
Sorting	Students assign words to categories based on their similarities and differences.	***Categories:*** ways we talk, ways we commute, ways we act ***Words:*** *mumble, drive, hesitant, mutter, bike, outgoing, flamboyant, walk, reserved*
Semantic webbing	Graphically depicts how words are related and classified.	
Semantic feature analysis	Graphically demonstrates the relationships among concepts within categories.	*(see table below)*

	zoo	home	forest	farm	pet store
pig	–	–	–	+	–
dog	–	+	–	+	+
zebra	+	–	–	–	–
rabbit	–	+	+	+	+
bear	+	–	+	–	–

FIGURE 2.6. Activities for direct instruction of vocabulary.

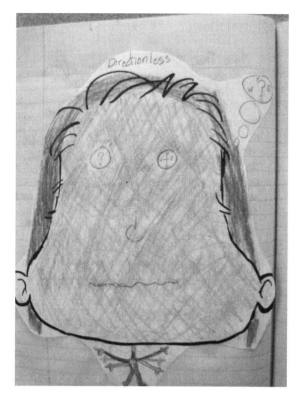

FIGURE 2.7. Fourth-grade student's visual representation of the word *directionless.*

> The work the children in these classrooms completed was more substantive and challenging and required more self-regulation than the work that has commonly been observed in elementary classrooms. We observed far less of the low-level worksheet-type tasks and found a greater reliance on more complex tasks across the school day and across subjects. Perhaps because of the nature of this work, students seemed more often engaged and less often off-task. (p. 745)

Built into long-term projects are many goals and strategies that accommodate differentiated learning to meet individual students' needs. Another aspect of long-term projects that contributes to student growth and engagement are the options available to students—options that accomplish the same goals and strategies but provide choice and ownership of learning. For example, in Julie's classroom, students worked on a 3-week poetry unit. Students had a poetry notebook in which they copied published poems they liked from their independent reading as well as poems they created. Students wrote poetry about topics of their own interest, which also reflected their self-selected independent reading choices. For instance,

World War II

Storming the beaches in Normandy
Departure Day in France
Men falling everywhere.

Mortar rounds exploding
Shrapnel flying everywhere
Thompson bullets never stopping.

Nazi troops never giving up
France slowly falling
Hitler has his revenge.

FIGURE 2.8. A poem written by a fourth grader.

in Figure 2.8, a fourth grader wrote a poem about World War II, which is not a part of the fourth-grade social studies curriculum in Virginia. The content and vocabulary reflect this student's interest in, and independent reading about, this period of history.

Poetry was integrated into science when students wrote poems about a science experiment in which they created bubbles while studying surface tension. Students wrote down their observations of surface tension, then wrote poems about their individual observations and experiences. As a culminating activity, parents were invited to a poetry tea at which students conducted a class performance of several published poems, and each child read a poem aloud of his or her own creation.

TALK ABOUT TEXTS

Lucy Calkins (2001) notes that "talk, like reading and writing, is a major motor—I could even say *the* major motor—of intellectual thinking" (p. 226). Though several recent studies have found that in the classrooms of highly effective teachers, real conversations take place regularly among students and between students and teachers, few teachers engage in classroom practices that promote such conversations or teach children how to talk about texts (Calkins, 2001; Cole, 2003; Ketch, 2005; Taylor & Pearson, 2002). Allington (2006) describes the differences between real-world literacy interactions and in-school literacy interactions and points out why providing an environment for genuine classroom talk is so important:

> When you consider the richness of the talk about texts that occurs outside of school, the typical pattern of school talk about texts seem shallow and barren. Outside school we rely on the richness of a person's conversation about texts to judge how well they understood it. Their literateness. In school we typically rely on the flat recitation of events or information to make that same judgment. Outside of school settings we engage in conversations about the adequacy of texts and authors to inform, engage, and entertain us. In school we engage in interrogations about what was "in the text." (p. 111)

By fostering peer and collaborative learning experiences, equity, community, and access to other students' thinking processes can be achieved. During teacher–student dialogues about text, the teacher should allow for student input and control and accept multiple interpretations of texts. Students' individual interpretations push others to think differently, to pose questions, or to make a hypothesis, thus broadening and deepening understanding. Teachers must resist approaches that stress the "true, accurate meaning" of the story. Ketch (2005) writes: "Conversation is a basis for critical thinking. It is the thread that ties together cognitive strategies and provides students with the practice that becomes the foundation for reading, writing, and thinking" (p. 8). Students need opportunities to practice the use of cognitive strategies in order to internalize them and strengthen their comprehension. Students who engage in conversation in the classroom become intellectually engaged with text (Kucan & Beck, 2003).

Authentic discussions can be built into many parts of the instructional day, such as before, during, and after read-aloud, shared reading, literature circles, and content-area learning. Electronic discussion via e-mail, bulletin boards, listservs, and Web logs (i.e., blogs) are another way to foster authentic conversation. Electronic discussion not only enables interaction and collaboration but also promotes reflection. Reading and responding to peers' comments compels us to think and to form and articulate ideas in a meaningful way. Reading peers' thoughts urges us to compare them with our own thoughts and ideas and, in turn, to examine our own understandings and interpretations.

WHAT WE KNOW ABOUT EFFECTIVE FOURTH-GRADE TEACHERS

This chapter outlined the challenges and exemplary practices of fourth-grade teachers in classrooms where children from diverse backgrounds are achieving high levels of literacy learning. The following list is a summary of these exemplary practices and can serve as a guideline for instructional planning:

1. Avoid the use of scripted programs, standardized lessons, and test preparation materials to prepare students for state-mandated testing. Rely on good instruction that meets individual student needs. This approach not only prepares students for enhanced test performance but eases test anxiety.

2. Teach students strategies for reading and learning from nonfiction and content-area textbooks; the lack of such strategies is one reason some students struggle with literacy in fourth grade.

3. Provide differentiated instruction that moves each student's literacy learning forward.

4. Use the *Standards for English Language Arts* along with state and local curriculum guides as a framework for integrated language instruction.

5. Providing ample time for students to read independently every day sends a strong message that reading is important and valued in the classroom. It also gives students the opportunity to orchestrate the skills and strategies they have learned during instruction and to acquire new knowledge and vocabulary. Students should also be allowed to self-select books of interest to them.

6. Stock the classroom library with a variety of authentic texts, including nonfiction. Students are more likely to transfer skills and strategies taught during classroom instruction if they read real books for real reasons.

7. Provide explicit instruction in comprehension strategies, employing the gradual-release-of-responsibility model that starts with a high level of teacher scaffolding and slowly guides students to apply strategies independently. Demonstrating the use of multiple strategies simultaneously provides students with a realistic model of how good readers employ comprehension strategies.

8. Provide students with opportunities to learn new vocabulary incidentally through wide reading and explicitly through teacher-directed instruction. Multiple exposure to words in a variety of contexts will more likely ensure that students take ownership of words and strategies for figuring out new words.

9. Engage students in longer-term literacy projects that integrate the content-area curriculum. Long-term projects motivate and engage students while also meeting the multiple goals and strategies of individual learners.

10. Provide multiple and varied opportunities for students to engage in genuine conversations with each other and the teacher. Real conversations around meaningful topics enhance engagement and critical thinking.

According to NCLB, a "highly qualified teacher" is defined as having full certification, a bachelor's degree, and demonstrated competence in subject knowledge and teaching. Yet, a college degree and subject-matter knowledge does not necessarily produce a highly effective teacher, just as no single definition can capture the multifaceted, complex nature of exemplary fourth-grade teaching. Thus, the presentation of information in this chapter runs the risk of "listing" characteristics rather than capturing the *synergy* that happens between and within these characteristics during the act of teaching. The remaining chapters attempt to more fully develop these characteristics and the synergy created by outstanding fourth-grade teachers.

REFERENCES

Allington, R. (Ed.). (2002). *Big brother and the national reading curriculum: How ideology trumped evidence.* Portsmouth, NH: Heinemann.

Allington, R. (2006). *What really matters for struggling readers* (2nd ed.). New York: Longman.

Allington, R. L., & Johnston, P. H. (2002). *Reading to learn: Lessons from exemplary fourth-grade classrooms.* New York: Guilford Press.

Allington, R., Johnston, P., & Day, J. (2002). Exemplary fourth-grade teachers. *Language Arts, 79*(6), 462–466.

Bandura, A. (1997). Self-efficacy: Toward a unifying theory of behavioral change. *Psychological Review, 84,* 191–215.

Beck, I. L., McKeown, M. G., & Kucan, L. (2002). *Bringing words to life: Robust vocabulary instruction.* New York: Guilford Press.

Biemiller, A. (2001). Teaching vocabulary: Early, direct, and sequential. *American Educator, 25*(1), 24–28, 47.

Block, C. C., & Mangieri, J. N. (2003). *Exemplary literacy teachers: Promoting success for all children in grades K–5.* New York: Guilford Press.

Calkins, L. (2001) *The art of teaching reading.* Portsmouth, NH: Heinemann.

Chall, J., Jacobs, V., & Baldwin, L. (1990). *The reading crisis: Why poor children fall behind.* Cambridge, MA: Harvard University Press.

Cole, A. (2003). *Knee to knee, eye to eye: Circling in on comprehension.* Portsmouth, NH: Heinemann.

Cooter, R. (Ed.). (2003). *Perspectives on rescuing urban literacy education: Spies, saboteurs and saints.* Mahwah, NJ: Erlbaum.

Dorn, L., & Soffas, C. (2005). *Teaching for deep comprehension.* Portland, ME: Stenhouse.

Duke, N. (2000). 3.6 minutes per day: The scarcity of informational texts in first grade. *Reading Research Quarterly, 35,* 202–224.

Duke, N. (2004). The case for informational text. *Educational Leadership, 61*(6), 40–44.

Duke, N., & Pearson, P. D. (2002). Effective practices for developing reading comprehension. In A. Farstrup & S. J. Samuels (Eds.), *What research has to say about reading instruction* (3rd ed., pp. 205–242). Newark, NJ: International Reading Association.

Fielding, L., Kerr, N., & Rosier, P. (1998). *The 90% reading goal.* Kennewick, WA: National Reading Foundation.

Fielding, L., & Pearson, P. (1994). Reading comprehension: What works. *Educational Leadership, 51*(5), 62–68.

Fresch, M. (1995). Self-selection of early literacy learners. *The Reading Teacher, 49*(3), 220–227.

International Reading Association and National Council of Teachers of English. (1996). *Standards for the English language arts.* Newark, DE: International Reading Association

Johnson, D. (2008). *The joy of children's literature.* Boston: Houghton Mifflin.

Ketch, A. (2005). Conversation: The comprehension connection. *The Reading Teacher,* 59(1), 8–13.

Kragler, S., Walker, C., & Martin, L. (2005). Strategy instruction in primary content textbooks. *The Reading Teacher,* 59(3), 254–261.

Kucan, L., & Beck, I. (2003). Inviting students to talk about expository texts: A comparison of two discourse environments and their effects on comprehension. *Reading Research and Instruction,* 42, 1–29.

McLaughlin, M., & Allen, M. (2002). *Guided comprehension: A teaching model for grades 3–8.* Newark, DE: International Reading Association.

Nagy, W. (1988). *Teaching vocabulary to improve reading comprehension.* Urbana, IL: National Council of Teachers of English.

National Assessment of Educational Progress. (2000). Washington, DC: Department of Education.

National Center on Education and the Economy and the University of Pittsburgh. (2001). *Performance standards: Elementary.* Pittsburgh, PA: Author.

National Center for Education Statistics. (2004). *Digest of educational statistics.* Washington, DC: U.S. Department of Education Institute of Education Sciences. Retrieved January 30, 2007, from *www.nces.ed.gov/programs/digest/d04/tables/dt04_150.asp*

National Center for Education Statistics. (2005). *Digest of educational statistics.* Washington, DC: U.S. Department of Education Institute of Education Sciences. Retrieved January 30, 2007, from *www.nces.ed.gov/programs/digest/d05/tables/dt05_150.asp*

Pressley, M., Allington, R. L., Wharton-MacDonald, R., Block, C. C., & Morrow, L. M. (2001). *Learning to read: Lessons from exemplary first-grade classrooms.* New York: Guilford Press.

Purcell-Gates, V., Duke, N., & Martineau, J. (2007). Learning to read and write genre-specific text: Roles of authentic experience and explicit teaching. *Reading Research Quarterly,* 42(1), 8–45.

RAND Study Group. (2002). *Reading for understanding: Toward an R & D program in reading comprehension.* Arlington, VA: RAND.

Routman, R. (2003). *Reading essentials.* Portsmouth, NH: Heinemann.

Schlager, N. (1978). Predicting children's choices in literature: A developmental approach. *Children's Literature in Education,* 9(3), 136–142.

Snow, C., Burns, S., & Griffin, P. (1998). *Preventing reading difficulties in young children.* Washington, DC: National Academy Press.

Taylor, B., & Pearson, P. (2002). *Teaching reading: Effective schools, accomplished teachers.* Mahwah, NJ: Erlbaum.

Wharton-MacDonald, R., Pressley, M., & Hampston, J. (1998). Outstanding literacy instruction in first grade: Teacher practices and student achievement. *Elementary School Journal,* 99, 101–128.

Worthy, J. (1996). Removing barriers to voluntary reading for reluctant readers: The role of school and classroom libraries. *Language Arts,* 73(7), 483–492.

CHILDREN'S LITERATURE

Brink, C. (1973). *Caddie Woodlawn.* New York: Macmillan.

Cole, J. (1987). *Magic school bus.* New York: Scholastic.

Giovanni, N. (1973). *Ego-tripping and other poems for young people.* New York: Lawrence Hill.

Kramer, S. (2001). *Hidden worlds: Looking through a scientist's microscope*. Boston: Houghton Mifflin.

Lee, J. (1982). *Legend of the milky way*. New York: Holt, Rinehart, and Winston.

Lewis, C. S. (1960). *The lion, the witch and the wardrobe*. New York: Macmillan.

Rowling, J. K. (1998). *Harry Potter and the sorcerer's stone*. New York: Scholastic.

Sattler, H. (1981). *Dinosaurs of North America*. New York: Lothrop, Lee & Shepard.

CHAPTER 3

SETTING UP THE CLASSROOM ENVIRONMENT FOR LITERACY LEARNING

CHARACTERISTICS OF AN EFFECTIVE ENVIRONMENT FOR LITERACY LEARNING

> We'd like to think that we are working in such wise ways that our students will care about their own literacy long after they graduate. In fact, there is only one reason we work so hard to create such a beautiful and inviting literacy setting filled with extensive collections, schoolwide literacy rituals, and ways to keep up with children's literature. We want our students to make a lifelong commitment to reading and writing. And so we begin by painstakingly caring about the literacy landscape, and then we proceed to do the best literacy teaching imaginable. . . .
> —HARWAYNE (2000, p. 44)

The physical landscape of a classroom reflects the teacher's belief about how children learn. Imagine walking into a classroom in which the students' desks have been arranged into clusters of four facing each other. There is no teacher's desk, but there is a file cabinet and a cart with teaching supplies, books, and a laptop computer beside a small table and chairs at the back of the room. In one corner is a carpeted area with pillows, an end table with a lamp, and several bookcases filled with children's books. In another corner is a large carpeted area with an easel and chart paper. Student work is on the walls around the room. What does the physical description of this classroom tell you about the teacher's beliefs regarding student learning? This classroom reflects a student-oriented perspective in which:

> ➤ The space is geared primarily for student learning.
> ➤ Students learn from opportunities to talk, collaborate, and interact with each other.
> ➤ Books are accessible and selected and read independently by students.
> ➤ Student work is valued and can be used to facilitate collaborative learning.
> ➤ Whole-class and small-group instruction are both conducted to meet students' needs.

Though many teachers work in classrooms with less than desirable conditions, due to deteriorating buildings and limited space, outstanding teachers are still able to create an inviting, print-rich environment for learning. The physical arrangement of the room and the resources made available to students influence the overall social, intellectual, and emotional environment.

WHAT SHOULD A FOURTH-GRADE CLASSROOM LOOK LIKE?

Entering Julie's fourth-grade classroom, one can only describe the literacy landscape as buzzing with the excitement of learning. Children are scattered throughout the room working on projects individually and collaboratively. Students are eager to share their learning:

> ➤ One student is writing a letter to Julie, explaining why she should read *Dear Austin* by Elvira Woodruff (1998); it is about the Underground Railroad and he knows how much she loves reading about that.
> ➤ Two students are discussing their reading of *Bud, Not Buddy* by Christopher Paul Curtis (1999). One of the students doesn't agree with the other student's interpretation of an event in the book, so they reread the text together for clarification.
> ➤ Three students are engaged in writing and illustrating an event from *Bright Shadow* by Avi (1985) to share with their literature discussion group.

While students are engaged in individual and group activities, Julie is conferencing with a student about the book he is currently reading. Exemplary fourth-grade literacy teachers create lessons that establish many goals and strategies for each literacy activity and create several options from which students can choose to build their ability to assume responsibility for their learning when reading independently (Block & Mangieri, 2003). Julie's classroom is arranged in such a way as to facilitate the flow of students from one activity to another and to allow for individual, collaborative, and whole-class instruction. Students' desks are arranged in clusters of six, facing each other in the center of the room. In the back of the room is a table for small-group instruction. On one side of the room is a place for large-group meetings and instruction, and on the other side of the room is the library and reading area. On the walls are displays of students' work reflecting different topics of study. For example, one bulletin board contains index cards with examples of idioms written and illustrated by students from their independent reading (see Figure 3.1).

When asked to reflect on her classroom environment, Julie states:

"The fourth-grade classroom should reflect aspects of the curriculum that are either being studied or that are going to be studied. I like to see their work hanging on the walls after they have completed certain writing assignments. One thing I have found is that students love pictures about social studies topics. I guess it brings the people to life and makes them more interesting. Students will spend free time looking at characters of the Civil War, for instance. I also think the fourth-grade classroom needs to promote independence by having everything easily accessible for the students to get themselves. I like to have pillows for independent reading and a small table for group gatherings of book talks. A space for the whole class to gather is also a must. The most important component is the space for students to complete

FIGURE 3.1. An example of a fourth-grade student's illustrated idiom.

different types of activities. This gets to be a challenge when class sizes are increasing. We use our whole-class space also for mini-lessons, sharing of writing, and our read-alouds. This physical arrangement keeps everyone close and engaged."

The physical arrangement of Julie's classroom reflects her beliefs about literacy learning and facilitates students' opportunities to engage in meaningful literacy activities.

Creating Community

When students enter the classroom, they do not leave their personal, social, and cultural selves at the door. Children are members of families, neighborhoods, religious groups, sports teams, clubs, and organizations, each of which is a community of practice. "Communities of practice are places where human beings *develop competence through their interactions* with each other" (Crafton, 2006, p. 1). Through these interactions, we define our identities. Classrooms are also communities of practice wherein each student possesses unique knowledge and perspectives that push the thinking of every other student.

Supportive classroom communities of practice accomplish the following:

➤ Allow students to develop positive identities about themselves as learners.

➤ Foster the learning of new interactions while also honoring existing ones.

➤ Create opportunities for students to contribute their past experiences to the collective knowledge of the group.

Fourth-grade students bring many experiences to the classroom, and excellent fourth-grade teachers create communities of practice that allow them to personalize instruction in ways that help students better understand how literacy can help them live a fulfilling and successful life. After only a short time in Julie's classroom, it is clear that creating community among herself and her students is a priority. Julie relates:

"From the beginning I work with a new class on the concept that we are all in this together. I think getting to know each others' strengths and weaknesses is an important part. I have had inclusion students who are excellent in history, and the class looks up to them and respects their knowledge. Another student with many challenges was actually very theatrical. The students loved to see him perform in Readers' Theatre and actually requested him to be in their group. Of course, they all know there are certain areas in which each of them struggles. But, by helping them to shine in some areas, respect is built. Humor about myself and them is always a part of my classroom community. If we can all laugh at ourselves, then some stress is relieved. For instance, my students know that my drawing is terrible, and we all laugh at it. So, hopefully knowing our strengths and understanding our weaknesses helps us to all work together and get along. I also like them to work together from early on to get to know how to share ideas and work together. I always change group composition, so there is never one set of partners—which helps students to get to know one another."

When teachers develop classroom communities of practice in which students respect the knowledge and contributions of each other, they help children understand that learning isn't just about "doing more school" but is about participating in something that matters to them.

Selecting Books/Media and Organizing the Classroom Library

As discussed in Chapter 2, an important feature of the classroom context that supports the development of good readers is providing students with access to varied and authentic texts. Providing a collection that reflects a range of student interests, preferences, genres, and curricular resources is critical to students' motivation—a primary concern of many fourth-grade teachers. Pachtman and Wilson (2006) surveyed 22 fourth-grade students to find out which components of the reading program were most beneficial in motivating them to read. The proximity of the classroom library and access to its large number of books were rated as very important by an overwhelming majority of students. Edmunds and Bauserman (2006) conducted interviews with 91 fourth-graders to find out what motivated them to read. Analysis of the interviews revealed six factors that increased children's motivation to read: (1) self-selection of books, (2) access to a variety of fiction and nonfiction books, (3) access to books that are personally interesting, (4) access to lots of books, (5) being read to by teachers and family members, and (6) when peers shared what they were reading with them. Thus, for the classroom library to play an integral role in children's literacy motivation and development, it must be far more than merely a place to store books. Careful consideration must be given to the purpose and function of the library.

According to Reutzel and Fawson (2002), a well-stocked and designed library can:

➢ Support literacy instruction.

➢ Help students learn about books.

➢ Provide a central location for classroom resources.

➢ Provide opportunities for independent reading and curricular extensions.

➢ Serve as a place in which students can talk about, and interact with, books.

How the classroom library is organized can help children learn about book choice. Answers to the following list of questions can serve as a guideline for setting up an inviting and effective classroom library at the beginning of each year (Sibberson & Szymusiak, 2003, p. 14):

➢ How can the classroom library support good book-choice habits? How can it support children as they think about themselves as readers, find favorite authors, and read for different purposes?

➢ Will the entire classroom library be located in one area of the room or will different sections be placed in different parts of the room?

➢ Will nonfiction be in a different area from fiction? How will separate locations help children learn why they read different genres?

➢ To what type of reading materials will students have access during reading time? Will they be encouraged to read magazines, news articles, comic books, poetry?

➢ How will I find space to display books face-out?

➢ Which displays will be permanent? Which will include rotating titles?

➢ Will I use baskets to organize books by the same authors, topics, and genre?

➢ How will I highlight less popular books to make them appealing to students?

➢ How will I make room to highlight books throughout the year based on students needs?

Julie explains how she selects books:

"My bookshelves are full of a variety of books. I like to put them in baskets by subject because it helps when looking for books. I also think books should be rotated so that there are always new books on different topics. For instance books that are more appropriate for certain seasons or books about different curriculum units are offered as new books. I also have nonfiction baskets and magazines to meet students' interests and preferences. I really like it when it's time to put a new basket of books on the bookshelf. The excitement is contagious!"

The reading attitude/interest inventory Julie administered at the beginning of the year (discussed in Chapter 1) provided her with an idea of the types of books that would be of interest to the students. She began the year by stocking her classroom library with books and magazines about fantasy, adventure, comics, and various sports. As the year progressed and the students' interests grew and changed, she selected new books that included historical fiction, nonfiction books about topics studied in social studies and science, and biographies.

Book baskets can be an effective and flexible way to organize books. They can be easily labeled and moved around for browsing. Baskets provide a means for displaying books in a way that maximizes students' exposure to new authors, genres, and topics (see Figures 3.2 and 3.3).

A study by Williams and Bauer (2006) found that teachers did not include children's literature in their classroom to better meet the literacy needs of students due to (1) a lack of time, (2) uncertainty of where to find books, (3) not knowing about books that would be appropriate for both their students and the curriculum, and (4) an inability to align children's books with objectives assessed on the state high-stakes test (p. 15). Many organizations are dedicated to providing teachers and children with information about quality literature, and access to these resources on the Internet can make the task of finding appropriate books that meet curriculum objectives less time consuming. Chapter 8 lists links to the Newbery and Caldecott Award winners along with other book awards and notable book lists by such organizations as the National Council of Teachers of Social Studies and the National Science Teacher's Association. The International Reading Association's Children's, Young Adult, and Teacher's Choices awards are also a great source for book recommendations. These books are voted on annually and the winners are listed in *The Reading Teacher* or are available online (*www.reading.org*). A list of graphic novels, magazines, and online books is provided in Figure 3.4.

INSTRUCTIONAL PRACTICES
FOR ACHIEVING LITERACY GOALS

Fourth-grade teachers must utilize highly effective instructional practices in order to meet the diverse literacy needs of their students, while also effectively teaching them how to extract information from a textbook, apply strategies beyond literature to content areas, and employ comprehension strategies and critical thinking to the content areas. Excellent fourth-grade teachers employ flexible instructional practices that allow them to move up or down the cognitive scale instantly to adapt to students' needs.

Reading Aloud

Does reading aloud to students make a difference? Oh, you bet it does. When we read aloud to children, we fill the air and their ears with the sound of language. Reading aloud to students (of all ages) invites them to make meaning, create images, and linger with language—to become infatuated with words and simply fall into a story.

—LAMINACK AND WADSWORTH (2006, p. 1)

Curriculum topics	Authors' names
Genres and subgenres such as mysteries, sports, graphic novels, and memoirs	Favorite series books
Magazines and comics	Teacher recommendations
Students' recommendations	Favorite characters
Award-winning books	Books written by students in the class
Books with memorable language	Funny books

FIGURE 3.2. Example of ways to categorize books.

FIGURE 3.3. Books categorized by topic.

GRAPHIC NOVELS

Akiko Pocket Size (Vols. 1–5) by Mark Crilley (Sirius Entertainment)

Alison Dare: Little Miss Adventures (Vols. 1–2) by J. Torres and J. Bone (Oni Press)

Hikaru No Go (Vols. 1–9) written by Yumi Hotta and illustrated by Takeshi Obata (VIZ Media LLC)

Bone (Vols. 1–5) by Jeff Smith (Cartoon Books)

Amelia Rules! (Vols. 1–3) by Jim Gownley (Renaissance Press)

Graphic Myths and Legends series by Steve Kurth (Graphic Universe)

MAGAZINES

American Girl (*www.americangirl.com/agmg/index.html*)

Boys' Quest (*www.boysquest.com*)

Cricket (*www.cobblestonepub.com/magazine/CKT*)

Calliope World History for Young People (*www.cobblestonepub.com/magazine/CAL*)

Highlights Magazine (*www.highlights.com*)

Jack and Jill (*www.jackandjillmag.org*)

Muse (*www.cobblestonepub.com/magazine/MUS*)

National Geographic News for Kids (*www.nationalgeographic.com/ngkids*)

Nickelodeon Magazine (*www.nick.com/all_nick/nick_mag*)

Ranger Rick (*www.nwf.org/gowild*)

Skipping Stones: An International Multicultural Magazine (*www.skippingstones.org*)

Stone Soup (*www.stonesoup.com*)

Sports Illustrated for Kids (*www.sikids.com*)

Time for Kids (*www.timeforkids.com/TFK*)

U.S. Kids (*www.uskidsmag.org*)

ONLINE BOOKS

The Nightmare Room by R. L. Stine (*www.thenightmarerrom.com*)

New Year's Eve by Martha Burnett (*web.mac.com/marta.burnett1*)

Gecko and Sticky by Wendelin Van Draanen (*libcat.mcldaz.org/gecko*)

Inanimate Alice by Kate Pullinger (*www.inanimatealice.com*)

The Neddiad by Daniel Pinkwater (*www.pinkwater.com/theneddiad*)

FIGURE 3.4. Graphic novels, magazines, and online books appropriate for fourth grade.

From *Teaching Literacy in Fourth Grade* by Denise Johnson. Copyright 2008 by The Guilford Press. Permission to photocopy this figure is granted to purchasers of this book for personal use only (see copyright page for details).

According to Jim Trelease, author of *The Read Aloud Handbook* (1993), "Human beings—be they five-year-olds or fifty-five-year-olds—will only do over and over what brings them pleasure" (p. xii). How do teachers make the pleasure connection with students who struggle with reading or who may be "turned off" to reading? The answer is reading aloud! *Becoming a Nation of Readers*, a report from the Commission on Reading, states, "The single most important activity for building the knowledge required for eventual success in reading is reading aloud to children. . . . There is no substitute for a teacher who reads children good stories. . . . It is a practice that should continue throughout the grades" (Anderson, Hiebert, Scott, & Wilkinson, 1984, p. 51). Unfortunately, for many students, being read to by a teacher stops after the primary grades. Yet, reading aloud to older students results in increased motivation and engagement (Holdaway, 1979; Ivey & Broaddus, 2001), vocabulary development and listening comprehension (Dickinson & Smith, 1994; Elley, 1989; Feitelson, Kita, & Goldstein, 1986), and language and literary development (Phillips & McNaughton, 1990; Sipe, 2000; Sulzby, 1985). When discussion is part of the read-aloud experience, students learn how to respond to literature and participate in literary discussion. According to Daniels and Zemelman (2004),

> Reading aloud evokes the time-honored human experience of listening to stories, telling family and cultural histories, trading "war stories," hearing lessons from elders—around a fire, at the dinner table, in family gatherings, at business conferences, wherever people meet in groups. It helps students grasp the big ideas, fascinations, and questions that make our subjects meaningful to us as thoughtful adults. Good teachers have learned that reading strong writing aloud draws in students who would otherwise resist engaging in school topics. (p. 110)

Though a variety of texts can be read aloud—including newspaper and magazine articles, short stories, and chapter books—picture books may be one of the best resources. "Although many intermediate and middle school teachers do not consider using them because they believe they are for younger children, numerous picture books are better suited for older readers, because they address more mature issues" (Albright, 2002, p. 419). Picture books are short and can be completed within a single class period, they provide a variety of uses for instruction, and they promote visual literacy. Visual literacy—the ability to discriminate and interpret images—is increasingly important as visual images play a dominant role through the Internet, television, and print media in our society. As we enter the information age, the adage "a picture is worth a thousand words" suggests the power of images.

Reading a picture book aloud may seem like a simple act, but many intentional decisions must go into the read-aloud experience to make it a meaningful event that supports literacy development (Morrow & Brittain, 2003). Teachers may choose books that lend themselves to teaching certain strategies. Harvey and Goudvis (2000) point out, "Realistic fiction and memoirs often spur connections and questions in readers. Poetry is likely to stimulate visualizing and inferential thinking. We frequently choose nonfiction pieces to teach determining importance and synthesizing information when we read" (p. 53). The following list provides additional guidelines for choosing texts to read aloud. Choose texts that

➢ are developmentally appropriate and sustain readers emotionally and intellectually,

➢ evoke a range of aesthetic responses and connect to children's lives,

➢ are of high literary quality and include believable characters, engaging plots, memorable language, and universal themes, and

➢ meet all of the above criteria and have relevant curricular connections.

Once the read-aloud book has been selected, it's time to share it with the students. It is critical to hold the book so all can see the pictures. Communicate the mood and meaning of the story and characters through vocal variation and pace, body position, eye expression, and contact. Julie discusses how she chooses and utilizes read-alouds:

> "The read-aloud is an excellent source for talk about reading workshop topics because all students have read the book. The read-aloud book provides an opportunity to reinforce vocabulary and comprehension strategies such as predicting, inferencing, cause–effect, sequencing, and character development I choose the read-aloud books to coordinate with some of the curriculum. Historical fiction is a component of our curriculum, so we read books that go along with some of our units (e.g., Revolutionary War, Civil War). However, I don't want to overemphasize one genre. I read fantasy and realistic fiction books, too. I think the students enjoy the variety of genres and the connections to curriculum. For the most part, the read-aloud books are not popular titles the students have read. They will explore authors after the read-aloud and look for other books by that person. Sometimes we have a follow-up activity after we finish the book. Maybe it's the movie version to compare and contrast or an activity mentioned in the book. If I miss the read-aloud, the class gets very upset and reminds me."

Teachers can model engagement and use of reading strategies during reading aloud by sharing their thoughts through think-alouds, described in the next section.

THINKING ALOUD

Thinking aloud while reading aloud can make the invisible processes of reading visible. For example, figuring out unknown words by the context or making inferences between what the author states and what the reader knows are complex processes that take place while reading text. Thinking aloud occurs when the teacher models his or her thinking by voicing all the things he or she notices, sees, feels, or questions while processing the text: "Think-alouds allow all students to hear how others sleuth out and make sense of all these text clues so that they can recognize and adopt these strategies as their own" (Wilhelm, 2001, p. 19).

According to Wilhelm (2001, p. 28), think-alouds can be used to model:

➤ General processes of reading, like predicting, monitoring, and summarizing

➤ Task-specific processes like symbolism, irony, or bar graphs

➤ Text-specific processes like understanding the structure of an argument and evaluating its effectiveness

Think-alouds can be conducted with a variety of genres and texts, including newspaper articles, magazines, and Internet sites, which are all primarily nonfiction. Teachers can record think-alouds on chart paper or overheads to create a record of the strategies modeled so that students can refer to the charts later and make connections to other texts. Once students have observed the think-aloud process with a particular strategy numerous times, the teacher can turn over the process to them, to practice on their own. Children can use sticky notes to record their thinking for sharing with the teacher in conferences or with a peer.

Read-Aloud for Writers

> I believe reading aloud is probably the single most important teaching tool I have at my disposal, particularly for the teaching of writing.
>
> —RAY (2005, p. 1)

The benefits of reading aloud listed previously come about when children listen to the read-aloud with their reading selves. But, as Ray (2005) points out, their writing selves are also present, listening in. When children "allow their writing selves to listen to the read aloud with the attention equal to that of their reading selves . . . they will open up for themselves vast storehouses of knowledge about, particularly, what good writing *sounds* like" (p. 70). Authors have much to offer teachers in their quest to assist students on the journey to becoming good writers. But, how is this done? How do teachers assist children to learn to write from authors? Lucy Calkins (1994) points out that in order for good books to play a strong role in improving the quality of writing, the reading–writing connection must be nurtured in classrooms. This can be accomplished by the following:

➤ Invite students to know a book or an author so well that the book or author stands a chance of affecting even their writing.

➤ Help students match their writing and their reading.

➤ Pay attention to the reading–writing connections our students are already making.

➤ Help students realize that the effects of literature are achieved because of an author's deliberate craftsmanship. (p. 274)

The role of the teacher in each of the actions listed serves as an important scaffold in the process of children learning to apprentice themselves to authors. They are not necessarily steps to be taken and are interactive and recurring. When reading aloud, pause to think aloud about the author's use of words and well-crafted phrases and how this crafting influences the reader's understanding of the story.

Shared Reading

Shared reading was developed by Don Holdaway (1979) in an effort to simulate the "lap reading" experience that some children have at home, when, on a parent's lap, they are close enough to see the text and illustrations while hearing a caring adult read aloud and demonstrate the conventions of reading. In the classroom, shared reading provides an apprenticeship environment for the teacher to support children at various levels of reading development. Shared reading involves the use of enlarged text so that children can see the words and illustrations. Whereas reading aloud exposes children to books that might be above their reading level, shared reading directly involves children with reading text that they can read with the teacher's support. Big books and other enlarged texts cross all topics and content subjects. For example, shared reading of nonfiction texts can serve as a way for students to learn about science, social studies, or math as well as a way to learn to read a variety of informational text structures with the teacher's support. The guidelines shown in Figure 3.5 can be used in the selection of big books for older readers.

Once the text has been selected, the teacher reads it, modeling strategies that support students' needs, as determined by assessment and curricular objectives. The enlarged text allows the teacher to visibly and explicitly scaffold students' understanding of complex reading strategies, such as word-attack and comprehension strategies and identifying text structure and literary elements.

Eldredge, Reutzel, and Hollingsworth (1996) compared the effects of 10 minutes of daily shared reading to 10 minutes of round-robin reading practice on second-grade readers' fluency, accuracy, vocabulary acquisition, and comprehen-

Select quality literature that has the following characteristics:

- Is highly engaging, informative, and meaningful.
- Connects to students' interests, needs, culture, and curriculum.
- Has print that is large enough to read up to 15 feet away.
- Is close to the reading level of most of the students.
- Contains elements that support fluent reading.
- Contains elements that lend themselves to demonstration and deeper understanding, such as a table of contents, index, maps, diagrams, charts, a glossary, and illustrations with captions found in informational books.
- Lends itself to comprehension, higher-level thinking, and critical reading.
- Connects to other texts.

FIGURE 3.5. Guidelines for selecting big books for shared reading.

From *Teaching Literacy in Fourth Grade* by Denise Johnson. Copyright 2008 by The Guilford Press. Permission to photocopy this figure is granted to purchasers of this book for personal use only (see copyright page for details).

sion. They found that the shared book experience produced statistically superior results on all measures of reading proficiency. In a survey of over 600 middle and high school students, Allen (2000) found that shared reading was cited as the reason for the greatest gains in reading achievement. Numerous studies have shown that a critical factor in shared book reading is the interactive talk that takes place between the teacher and the children (Crain-Thoreson & Dale, 1992; DeTemple, 2001; Dickinson, 2001a, 2001b; Dickinson & Smith, 1994; Wasik & Bond, 2001).

The effectiveness of shared reading depends on (1) the selection of an appropriate text, (2) modeling strategies derived from the teacher's knowledge of students' reading strengths and needs, and (3) the teacher's ability to provide flexible scaffolding during students' reading.

Guided Reading

Because all children develop the skills and strategies of good readers at different rates, it is important for them to receive instruction that builds on their particular strengths and needs. Research has shown small-group instruction to be a critical component of effective instruction. Allington and Johnston (2002) observed 30 fourth-grade teachers from five states and found that the most effective classrooms implemented small-group instruction. In guided reading, teachers meet with small groups of students who are similar in their reading behavior, text-processing needs, and reading strengths. Instruction focuses on specific aspects of the reading process and literary understanding that will assist the children in moving forward to independence.

Guided reading is based on dynamic grouping according to students' strengths and needs; group compositions change as students' strengths and needs change. Through the orchestration of instructional decisions based on ongoing assessment, students continually grow toward reading independence.

Guided reading follows the gradual-release-of-responsibility model. The teacher selects an appropriate text (see Figure 3.6) based on students' strengths and needs and prepares an introduction to the text based on the support students' will need to read the text easily. Responsibility is then turned over to the students to read the text silently and individually. As the students read, the teacher observes and monitors their reading behaviors and provides support, as necessary. After reading, the teacher engages the students in talking about the story in a manner that is determined by his or her observations of students' needs. The lesson may include a follow-up activity. Figure 3.7 provides an overview of the components of a guided reading lesson.

While meeting with your guided reading group, the other children may be engaged in learning centers or reading independently. It is critical for every minute of the brief 15–20 minutes you have with your guided reading groups to be spent engaged in purposeful activity with those students and not interrupted by other students in the class. The first several weeks of school, when the teacher is assessing students prior to forming guided reading groups, is a perfect time to explicitly teach students what is expected when they participate in centers and independent reading. Write expectations on chart paper so that students can refer to them, as necessary. It is important that the activities in which students engage while away from the teacher are as powerful as when they are with the teacher.

- Leveled stories within basal readers
- Sets of trade books
- Sets of leveled books
- *Weekly Reader*, *Scholastic News*, or other nonfiction magazines
- Internet sites
- Poetry
- Nonfiction texts, including content-area books
- Writing aloud and shared writing texts

FIGURE 3.6. Texts that can be used for guided reading.

From *Teaching Literacy in Fourth Grade* by Denise Johnson. Copyright 2008 by The Guilford Press. Permission to photocopy this figure is granted to purchasers of this book for personal use only (see copyright page for details).

Before the reading	During the reading	After the reading
• Teacher selects an appropriate text that will be supportive but with a few manageable challenges. • Teacher prepares an introduction to the story. • Teacher briefly introduces the story, keeping in mind the meaning, language, and visual information in the text, and the knowledge, experience, and skills of the reader. • Teacher leaves some questions to be answered through the reading. • Students engage in a conversation about the story, raising questions, building expectations, and/or noticing information in the text.	• Teacher listens as the students read the whole text or a unified part to themselves (softly or silently). • Teacher observes and documents individual reader's strategy use. • Teacher interacts with individuals to assist with problem solving at points of difficulty (when appropriate). • Students request help in problem solving when needed.	• Teacher talks about the story with the children, inviting personal response. • Teacher returns to the text for one or two teaching opportunities, such as finding evidence or discussing problem solving. • Teacher assesses children's understanding of what they read. • Teacher sometimes engages the children in extending the story through such activities as drama, writing, art, or more reading. • Teacher may engage students in rereading the story to a partner or independently.

FIGURE 3.7. Essential elements of guided reading. From Fountas and Pinnell (1996, p. 7). Copyright 1996 by Heinemann. Adapted by permission.

Reading Workshop

A reading workshop is an organizational framework in which children are actively engaged in reading, responding, discussing, and sharing books with the teacher and peers. The teacher conducts a brief book talk, followed by a mini-lesson determined by students' strengths and needs and curricular goals, and then confers with individual students during independent reading time. Figure 3.8 is a sample breakdown of one hour of time within a reading workshop. A brief discussion of those components follow.

5–15 minutes	Book talks (occasionally) Mini-lessons
30–45 minutes	Individual reading Conferring Written response
5–10 minutes	Group sharing

FIGURE 3.8. Schedule for a 1-hour reading workshop.

Book Talks

A book talk is a 1- to 2-minute presentation prepared by teachers or students as a way to entice others to read a particular book. The presenter provides the title, author, and brief summary of the book and then explains why he or she liked it and why other students might be interested in it. A short excerpt may be read aloud and a few illustrations shown. The book can then be displayed on a chalk tray or shelf to encourage students to read it.

Regie Routman (2003) uses book talks as a way to demonstrate to students how she chooses books to read:

> Recommendations from friends and book reviews are my main sources for deciding what to read. I read *The New York Times Book Review* every Sunday, clip book reviews, and earmark books I want to read. But mostly, I rely on friends for trusted recommendations. . . . I also keep a folder of "Books I Want to Read." When I hear or read about a book I might want to read or clip an intriguing book review, I place it inside the folder. (p. 31)

Book talks are a great way for teachers to model their own love of reading while introducing students to quality children's literature.

Mini-Lessons

A mini-lesson is a brief, powerful, explicit teaching point at the beginning of a reading workshop that clearly demonstrates a principle or process to students. In determining the focus of a mini-lesson, teachers draw upon students' needs as determined from reading conferences, observations, and curricular goals. Mini-lessons fall into three categories:

1. *Procedures and organization.* Early in the school year, the management of reading workshop is most important for successful independent reading. These mini-lessons might focus on respecting the learning of others, how to buddy-read, or how to select a "just right book."

2. *Reading strategies and skills.* Based on assessment information, these mini-lessons are designed to help children become aware of information in a text and learn how to understand and use that information to become a better reader. Mini-lessons might focus on how to problem-solve the meaning of unknown words, comprehension strategies, characteristics of texts (e.g., the organization of narrative and expository texts), and reading with fluency.

3. *Literary analysis.* Based on assessment information, these mini-lessons are designed to help children become familiar with crafting techniques and devices authors use to create quality literature. Mini-lessons might focus on story elements such as characterization, setting, and plot, making connections to the text and between texts, understanding the author's perspective, and critically analyzing texts for bias.

Mini-lessons on a specific principle or process will usually last a week or sometimes longer, depending on the teacher's ongoing observations of students' internalization of the principle or process. Calkins (2001) suggests that teachers design mini-lessons with the following question in mind: " *How* will I teach this content in ways that make a lasting impact?" (p. 84). Another good question to ask is "What will this instruction look like tomorrow?" Designing mini-lessons with these questions in mind keeps students' needs in the forefront of planning.

For example, understanding the author's point of view or perspective is an important comprehension strategy, especially as the books read by fourth graders become increasingly complex. Julie conducted a mini-lesson on perspective using the book *Katie's Trunk* by Ann Turner (1992). The story takes place during the period between the Boston Tea Party and the battles that began the American Revolution. Katie's family is not sympathetic to the rebel soldiers during the American Revolution, a perspective not presented in most social studies textbooks about this time period. When a group of armed neighbors comes to their home with the intention of stealing and looting, the family takes refuge in the adjoining woods—but Katie runs back to the house to protect their valuable possessions. She hides in a truck to keep from being discovered by the rebels. As Julie read the book aloud to the students, she stopped periodically to allow them to draw on their knowledge of the time period, make connections to their own thoughts and feelings about the events, and make predictions about how Katie and her family would deal with their situation. Julie ends the lesson by talking about the perspective taken by the author and how that affects the readers understanding of the story. Julie will follow this mini-lesson with subsequent mini-lessons on perspective and discuss the use of perspective with individual students during conferences.

Independent Reading/Conferences

While most children are reading independently, the teacher works one-on-one with individual students everyday in reading conferences to monitor their reading and provide specific feedback. By working with children individually, the teacher not only provides tailor-made feedback, but also gains an understanding of how children are applying the skills and strategies previously taught, thus informing future instruction. During reading conferences, the teacher's role is to:

➢ Engage in authentic conversations with the child about the texts he or she is reading.

➢ Help the child understand the routines involved in independent reading (i.e., self-selecting "just right" books, reading for a sustained period of time).

➢ Teach the child effective reading skills and strategies.

➢ Observe the student's oral reading to verify fluency and phrasing.

➢ Occasionally discuss the student's journal responses.

When Julie conferences with her students, she uses a conference sheet that allows her to make notes about each child (see Chapter 4). The following is an example of a conference Julie had with Rodney, who is reading *Mr. Lincoln's Drummer* (Wisler, 1995) (historical fiction). As Julie sits down beside Rodney in the corner of the room where he has been reading independently, she asks him to tell her about the story up to the part he is currently reading. This is Julie's first conference with Rodney since he started reading this book; he is on page 52. Julie notes that Rodney's retelling lacked important details: He couldn't remember the main character's name and wasn't sure of the story's setting. Julie then connected the story to a mini-lesson she had taught previously on setting and its importance to historical fiction. Next she prompted Rodney to look back in the story to find this information, and he quickly flipped to the beginning of the book, skimmed to the part he was looking for, and then read the section describing the time period to Julie. She then helped Rodney connect the information he had just read to the other details of the story he'd conveyed in the retelling. Julie then asked Rodney to read-aloud the next section in his book as she took a running record, noting on her conference sheet that he read the section fluently. After a brief discussion about this section, Julie engaged Rodney in making predictions about what might happen next. Then Julie moved on to another student.

Writing in Response to Reading

> When we write—we put our thinking onto the page—so we can hold onto our fleeting thoughts. When we write, we can hold our thoughts in our hand, we can put our thoughts in our pocket, and we can bring out yesterday's thoughts. When we write, we can give our thoughts to someone and combine our thoughts with someone else's

thoughts, and *we can improve our thoughts*. . . . When we write, we can look at our thinking and ask, "What's the really big idea here?" We can say, "What patterns do I see in my ideas?" We can ask, "How are your ideas like mine?" We can notice, "Things are changing!" (Calkins, 2001, p. 372)

Responding to reading through writing can be a great way for children to develop meaning since writing is reflection. However, for reading response to be a reflective process, children must be given the opportunity to write open-ended responses rather than to predetermined prompts and they must understand that there are many ways to respond that expand thinking about texts. One way to scaffold students' understanding of how to respond to reading is through the use of sticky notes. As you read aloud and model your own use of reading strategies through think-alouds, stop to write down your connections, questions, or predictions on sticky notes and place them on the appropriate pages in the book. After reading, go back and read the notes as a way of reflecting on your thinking about the book. Were your questions answered? Were your predictions correct? What thoughts or ideas would you like to talk about with a partner? Point out to students that your connections, questions, and predictions might be different than theirs and that each child will respond differently based on his or her experiences.

Sticky notes can be removed and placed on a page in a reading response journal and used as a scaffold for writing a response to the book in the reading response journal. A composition notebook or folder can be used as a reading response journal (see Figure 4.10 in Chapter 4 for an example of a student's response to reading). During reading workshop mini-lessons, model how to write responses to reading and provide many examples of journal entries over several weeks so they understand what you expect. Some teachers develop rubrics with scoring criteria that students use as a guideline (see Figure 4.11 in Chapter 4). Sticky notes and written responses are also very important for literature discussion groups. As students read, sticky notes become a reminder of what they want to talk about with their peers.

Students can record the date, title, and genre of all of the books they've read on a page attached to the inside front cover of the reading response journal. This provides the teacher and student with a quick way of seeing the breadth and depth of genre reading. A reading response journal provides the student with many ways to think about reading and provides the teacher with a source of information for assessing students' literary understanding.

Group Sharing

After independent reading time, it is important to bring the children together for a brief period to share their thinking about what and how they are reading and to evaluate how the students are working during independent reading. During this time, the teacher invites individuals to share what they are reading with the whole class or asks students to discuss with each other in groups of twos or threes. Book sharing creates an environment in which children learn from each other, a process that serves as a strong influence and motivator. Children give and take book recommendations, reinforce strategy use or literary understandings, make connections to previous learning, and broaden perspectives.

Book Clubs/Literature Circles

After reading a really good book, an informative newspaper article, or finding interesting information on the Internet, many adults seek out opportunities to engage in conversations with others to talk about the story or information that they enjoyed or found interesting. Comments and responses such as: "I loved the part . . . ", "I couldn't believe . . . ", "What did you think when . . . ?", "I don't agree with . . . ", "I wonder what happened when . . . " allow us to share our thoughts, perspectives, and insights and gain perspectives and insights from others. We make judgments about what we read and engage in conversations in which we agree, disagree, speculate, interpret, change our minds, and make connections with others that affect our thinking and our lives.

We don't engage in asking and answering a barrage of questions such as "Who were the main characters?", "Where was the setting?", "What was the problem?" If this were the way adults talked about books, then few, if anyone, would participate. However, this is the predominant way teachers engage children in talk about the books they read in school. Students learn that reading books is primarily to respond with the "right" answer during a recitation or on a worksheet. If that were the purpose of reading, how many books would you read? This practice of interrogating students for the purpose of evaluating their comprehension sends a strong message about the purpose of reading.

Book clubs or literature circles should be a time for students to come together in small groups to discuss their reading and allows them to engage in conversations about books that are directed by their own questions, thoughts, and perspectives. Based on 30 years of teaching experience, Ardith Cole (2003) writes, "Literature conversations provide a platform for deep, rich comprehension of text. By developing these classroom structures for talk, teachers can help students collaborate, substantiate their ideas, and negotiate" (p. xiv). Conversations about reading during read-alouds, shared reading, guided reading, and, to some extent, independent reading are teacher-directed. Though children will initially need teacher support, book clubs should eventually become student-directed and response-driven.

The selection of literature for discussion groups should be based on the teacher's knowledge of quality literature and students' interests, cultures, reading strengths and needs, independent reading levels, and cross-curricular goals. Interesting and relevant texts increase motivation and enhance discussions. Books can also be selected as part of a text set or books that are connected in some way. Ways to create text sets include:

➤ Student interests or suggested books

➤ Author/illustrator study

➤ Genre study

➤ Content connections

➤ Thematic study such as friendship, appreciating differences, or taking responsibility

➤ Books with multiple character perspectives

➤ Books with global perspectives

➤ Fiction/nonfiction pairs on the same topic

For example, one of the fourth-grade curriculum objectives for social studies in Virginia is to learn about the Jamestown settlement. If a fourth-grade teacher wanted her students to read historical fiction about this time period, she might choose the following text set:

➤ *A New Look at Jamestown* by Karen Lange (third grade)

➤ *Who's Saying What in Jamestown, Thomas Savage?* by Jean Fritz (fourth grade)

➤ *Blood on the River: Jamestown, 1607* by Elisa Carbone (fifth grade)

➤ *The Double Life of Pocahontas* by Jean Fritz (sixth grade)

These books represent a range of reading levels, perspectives, and issues during the founding of the Jamestown settlement that are developmentally appropriate for fourth graders. The teacher conducts a brief book talk on each of the books and then allows students to choose the book they want to read. A sign-up sheet can be used in which students indicate up to three different books they are interested in reading. Then the teacher decides who gets to read which books based on interest and reading level. The teacher should explain to students that not all students will get to read their first choice every time.

Literature discussion groups are heterogeneous with no more than five or six members based on books the students have chosen to read, though students who read different books on the same topic could form a discussion group. In the example above, all students are reading books about the Jamestown settlement. Students who have read each of the different books could form a group to talk about the different perspectives and issues discussed in the books. Students may have different reading abilities but are still able to engage in high-level discussion about topics they care about.

Though children participate daily in many conversations, often they are not about books. Thus, many children come to school without an understanding of what it is like to engage in a meaningful conversation about reading. Therefore, teachers may need to conduct mini-lessons on what is expected. Another excellent way to introduce students to book clubs is to show them a book club in action either live or through a video. If another teacher in your school implements book clubs, set up an opportunity for one of the groups to conduct a book club meeting in front of your students. Or, show students a video of students participating in a book club. The latter has the advantage of pausing to discuss the different interactions taking place between members of the group (examples of professional videos available are *Looking into Literature Circles* by Harvey Daniels and *Strategy Instruction in Action* by Stephanie Harvey and Anne Goudvis, both available at *www.stenhouse.com*). Based on mini-lessons and observations of book clubs in action, teachers can involve students in creating a list of "rules of engagement" in which students develop an initial list of what is important for book clubs to be effective. Additions and changes can be made to the list as students learn from their ongoing participation in book clubs.

Once students have decided on a book and a group is formed, an initial meeting is held with the teacher. Though the teacher has given a brief book talk that provided enough information for students to decide if they were interested in the book, there is still a need to build background knowledge, set a purpose for reading, and to decide how much to read before the first group discussion. The teacher might create a chart documenting students' prior knowledge, questions, and predictions that could be revisited during the first discussion group. Additionally, sometimes students get excited about reading a book and assign an unrealistic number of pages to be read before the first group meeting. The teacher can model how to judge an appropriate number of pages based on the number of days before the group meets and where a good stopping point might be in the book.

Over the next week students read the assigned pages during independent reading time. The students should be used to jotting down their thoughts on sticky notes and writing in response journals at this point. Students are reading with a new mindset—questions, thoughts, predictions, and critiques will be shared with discussion group members—that can open up a whole new way of thinking. The notes are critical to meaningful, thought-provoking discussion. Once the group has finished discussing the book, it is disbanded and new groups are formed for subsequent book clubs.

The following is an overview of considerations for teacher/student roles in book clubs:

Teacher's role:

➢ Select texts to be read

➢ Provide mini-lessons and model ways to have productive conversations

➢ Build students' prior knowledge

➢ Scaffold students' engagement in conversations about the text

➢ Slowly remove support and allow students to take responsibility

Students' role

➢ Read assigned pages

➢ Take notes about thoughts, questions, and ideas to discuss with book club members

➢ Come to the book club prepared and ready to participate

➢ Discuss ideas from sticky notes

➢ Be able to support thoughts and comments with the text

Writing Workshop

A writing workshop, like a reading workshop, is an organizational framework for independent writing. Time frames for the workshop components are noted in Figure 3.9.

Mini-Lessons

State or district standards and curriculum guides focus narrowly on skills in isolation, and the tendency might be to focus on these skills during mini-lessons. Yet, you will easily satisfy those minimum standards through meaningful teaching. Explicit teaching of skills and strategies should be a part of a quality writing program, but just as good readers do not use one reading strategy at a time, good writers do not focus on one writing strategy in isolation of others. "Teaching writing by focusing on the parts—spending weeks teaching sentence fluency or transitions or voice, for example—is not how writers work. Something is amiss in our writing classrooms when most of our time is spent on bits and pieces and exercises" (Routman, 2005, p. 15). In determining the focus of a mini-lesson, teachers draw upon students' needs, as determined from writing conferences and observations. Mini-lessons fall into three categories:

5–15 minutes	Mini-lesson
30–45 minutes	Individual writing Conferring
5–10 minutes	Group sharing

FIGURE 3.9. Time frames for writing workshop.

1. *Procedures and organization.* Focuses on the management of time, materials, equipment, and the inculcation of expectations for students to work both together and independently in writing workshop.

2. *Craft.* Focuses on learning to use a writer's notebook, revise, edit, publish, conduct research, write in different genres, develop a sense of audience, and learn from authors and illustrators.

3. *Conventions of writing.* Focuses on spelling, grammar, punctuation, paragraphing, and other writing conventions.

The significant questions to ask in creating meaningful mini-lessons in a writing workshop are the same as for a reading workshop: *How* will I teach this content in ways that make a lasting impact? and *What* will this instruction look like tomorrow? Designing mini-lessons with these questions in mind keeps students' needs in the forefront of planning. For example, Julie taught a mini-lesson on writing a good lead sentence for a story that would capture the attention of the reader and make him or her want to continue reading. She gathered several books that had powerful leads and shared them with her students, such as the first sentence of *Charlotte's Web* (White, 1952)—" 'Where's Pa going with that ax?' said Fern to her mother as they were setting the table for breakfast"—and the first sentence of *James and the Giant Peach* (Dahl, 1961)—"Until he was four years old, James Henry Trotter had a happy life." Each time she read aloud the first sentence of these familiar books, she discussed with the children why the lead was so powerful. Next, she divided the class into groups. Then she read a short story aloud and asked the groups to collaboratively write a new lead for the story. Each group then presented its lead and explained how it captured the reader and made him or her want to read more. As she dismissed students to begin independent writing, she asked them to think about writing exciting leads for their own stories.

Independent Writing/Conferences

While students are writing independently the teacher can meet with individual students. A writing conference is a brief, focused opportunity to move the child forward as a writer. With this goal in mind, rather than merely "fixing" a piece of writing, teachers make sure that students learn something that will help them become a better writer in the future. Keeping records of what is taught during conferences is critical to the student's progress over time. The teacher should meet with every student over the course of a week.

Recently, Julie asked the students to write fictional journal entries as if they were a person living during the Civil War. When she met with Holden about his journal entry, written from the perspective of Robert E. Lee, Julie asked Holden to read the entry aloud. This is the second time Julie has met with Holden about this journal entry. The first time, Julie helped Holden with the details; this time, Julie

```
May 27, 1864

Dear Journal,

   I love my horse Traveller. We have been together for
such a long time. I remember when I first bought him. I
bought him in the mountains of western Virginia; he was 5
years old then. He is 16 hands tall and taller than me. He
has a gray mane and tail. I immediately fell in love with
this horse because I could instantly see that he had a
good heart. I knew that this loyal steed would be my
friend from the beginning. Of all my four horses, he was
my favorite because of his loving character. I can see
that he is loved by all of my troops. I feel that I am
king of the world when I ride him. I rode him from Vir-
ginia to Georgia and then to Pennsylvania. I hope that
Traveller and I have many more hay memories.

   General Robert E. Lee
   Army of Northern Virginia
```

FIGURE 3.10. Holden's Civil War journal entry.

talks with Holden about the source of his information. Holden used *Robert E. Lee: Duty and Honor* (Hale, 2005) as a source of information for his entry. Julie reminded Holden of the mini-lesson she taught the previous week on the importance and format for citing sources of information. Together, they constructed the citation, and Holden wrote it on his rough draft. Later, Holden typed his entry (see Figure 3.10).

Group Sharing

Also called "author's chair," a brief period of time is provided for students after independent writing to share their work with each other. During group sharing children learn much about each other because they are also sharing their thinking. Writing always says something about the writer, which makes the sharing of writing a personal experience. After a child shares his or her writing with the class, the other children may offer praise and ask clarifying questions. The teacher can also use this time to provide the whole class with a chance to observe a writing conference in action: The teacher's interaction with the child during the group sharing can help them understand the types of questions to ask and feedback to offer during peer conferences.

Internet Workshop

In January 2008, the Library of Congress appointed author Jon Scieszka as the first National Ambassador for Young People's Literature. The position was created in collaboration with the Children's Book Council to raise national awareness of the importance of young people's literature as it relates to lifelong literacy, education, and the development and betterment of the lives of young people. In accepting this 2-year post, Scieszka chose to advocate for and focus on reaching reluctant readers—those children who are capable of reading but are not interested in reading. As part of his platform, Scieszka will offer suggestions on how to turn reluctant readers into avid readers. His suggestions include:

➢ Letting kids choose what they like and want to read.

➢ Expanding our definition of "reading" to include nonfiction, humor, graphic novels, magazines, action adventure, and Web content.

➢ Being good "reading" role models for children.

➢ Avoid demonizing TV, computer games, and new technologies.

Scieszka's suggestions for reaching reluctant readers embraces the diversity and breadth of children's literature available today, including the Internet and new technologies, which is important in connecting not only with reluctant readers but all children and young adults who will live and work in the 21st century.

Though fourth graders come to school equipped with prior experiences of using digital media, they do not necessarily know how to fully access and engage with them. Digital texts and information communication technologies (ICTs) are quickly becoming the predominant way people read and communicate at work and home. Teachers can use these tools to extend students' understanding, motivation, and engagement with children's literature in authentic ways that also extend opportunities to acquire the skills and strategies needed to live and work in the rapidly changing technological world.

The Internet workshop is an instructional framework developed by Don Leu (2002). Much like a reading/writing workshop, it is designed to help students understand the new literacies of the future. At the core of the new literacies is learning how to learn: "It is not just that we want students to know how to read and write; we want them to know how to continuously learn new skills and strategies required by the new technologies of literacy that will regularly emerge" (Leu, 2002, p. 467). An Internet workshop generally includes the following procedures:

1. Locate a site on the Internet that has content related to a classroom unit of instruction and set a bookmark for the location. This procedure ensures that the site is appropriate for the age and readability of the students and limits random surfing.

2. Design an activity, inviting students to use the site as they work on content, critical literacy, or strategic knowledge goals in your curriculum. (As students progress, you may also invite them to develop independent inquiry projects.) This step introduces students to the site and develops important background knowledge and navigation strategies for effective use of the Internet. The activity should be open-ended so that students have some inquiry options regarding the information that they will share at the end of the workshop.

3. Complete the research project. Assigning students to a schedule will assure that they have enough time during the week to complete the activity.

4. Have students share their work, questions, and new insights at the end of the week during a workshop session. You may also use this time to prepare students for the next workshop experience, which may extend opportunities to explore questions raised by, or interests emerging from, the previous workshop activity.

This framework can be used to explore many topics through simulations, WebQuests, and inquiry/Internet projects. In addition to content, students learn important critical literacy skills and strategies, such as how to conduct an effective search on the Internet; how to determine if information on the Internet is valid, reliable, and current; how to use the Internet to extend learning beyond traditional forms of information; and how the Internet and other ICTs allow communication with others around the world to broaden our perspectives and understanding.

REFERENCES

Albright, L. (2002). Bringing the ice maiden to life: Engaging adolescents in learning through picture book read-alouds in content areas. *Journal of Adolescent and Adult Literacy, 45*(5), 418–428.

Allen, J. (2000). *Yellow brick roads: Shared and guided paths to independent reading 4–12.* Portsmouth, ME: Stenhouse.

Allington, R. (2006). *What really matters for struggling readers: Designing research-based programs* (2nd ed.). Boston: Allyn & Bacon.

Allington, R. L., & Johnston, P. H. (2002). *Reading to learn: Lessons from exemplary fourth-grade classrooms.* New York: Guilford Press.

Anderson, R., Hiebert, E., Scott, J., & Wilkinson, I. (1984). *Becoming a nation of readers.* Champaign, IL: Center for the Study of Reading.

Block, C. C., & Mangieri, J. N. (2003). *Exemplary literacy teachers: Promoting success for all children in grades K–5.* New York: Guilford Press.

Calkins, L. (1994). *The art of teaching writing.* Portsmouth, NH: Heinemann.

Calkins, L. (2001). *The art of teaching reading.* Portsmouth, NH: Heinemann.

Cole, A. (2003). *Knee to knee, eye to eye: Circling in on comprehension.* Portsmouth, NH: Heinemann.

Crafton, L. (2006). What are communities of practice? Why are they important? *School Talk, 12*(1), 1–2.

Crain-Thoreson, C., & Dale, P. (1992). Do early talkers become early readers? Linguistic precocity, preschool language, and emergent literacy. *Developmental Psychology, 28,* 421–429.

Daniels, H., & Zemelman, S. (2004). *Subjects matter: Every teacher's guide to content-area reading.* Portsmouth, NH: Heinemann.

DeTemple, J. (2001). Parents and children reading books together, In D. K. Dickinson & P. O. Tabors (Eds.), *Beginning literacy with language* (pp. 31–51). Baltimore: Brookes.

Dickinson, D. (2001a). Book reading in preschool classrooms: Is recommended practice common? In D. K. Dickinson & P. O. Tabors (Eds.), *Beginning literacy with language* (pp. 175–203). Baltimore: Brookes.

Dickinson, D. (2001b). Putting the pieces together: Impact of preschool on children's language and literacy development in kindergarten. In D. K. Dickinson & P. O. Tabors (Eds.), *Beginning literacy with language* (pp. 257–287). Baltimore: Brookes.

Dickinson, D., & Smith, M. (1994). Long-term effects of preschool teachers' book readings on low-income children's vocabulary and story comprehension. *Reading Research Quarterly, 29,* 105–122.

Edmunds, K., & Bauserman, K. (2006). What teachers can learn about reading motivation through conversations with children. *The Reading Teacher, 59*(5), 414–424.

Eldredge, J., Reutzel, D., & Hollingsworth, P. (1996). Comparing the effectiveness of two oral reading practices: Round-robin reading and the shared book experience. *Journal of Literacy Research, 28*(2), 201–225.

Elley, W. (1989). Vocabulary acquisition from listening to stories. *Reading Research Quarterly, 24,* 174–187.

Feitelson, D., Kita, B., & Goldstein, Z. (1986). Effects of listening to series stories on first graders' comprehension and use of language. *Research in the Teaching of English, 20,* 339–356.

Fountas, I., & Pinnell, G. (1996). *Guided reading.* Portsmouth, NH: Heinemann.

Harvey, S., & Goudvis, A. (2000). *Strategies that work.* York, ME: Stenhouse.

Harwayne, S. (2000). *Lifetime guarantees.* Portsmouth, NH: Heinemann.

Holdaway, D. (1979). *The foundations of literacy.* Sydney, Australia: Ashton Scholastic.

Ivey, G., & Broaddus, K. (2001). "Just plain reading": A survey of what makes students want to read in middle school classrooms. *Reading Research Quarterly, 36*(4), 350–377.

Kucan, L., & Beck, I. (2003). Inviting students to talk about expository texts: A comparison of two discourse environments and their effects on comprehension. *Reading Research and Instruction, 42,* 1–29.

Laminack, L., & Wadsworth, R. (2006). *Learning under the influence of language and literature: Making the most of read-alouds across the day.* Portsmouth, NH: Heinemann.

Leu, D. (2002). Internet workshop: Making time for literacy. *The Reading Teacher, 55*(5), 466–472.

Morrow, L., & Brittain, R. (2003). The nature of storybook reading in elementary school: Current practices. In A. van Kleeck, S. Stahl, & E. Bauer (Eds.), *On reading books to children: Parents and teachers* (pp. 140–158). Mahwah, NJ: Erlbaum.

Pachtman, A., & Wilson, K. (2006). What do the kids think? *The Reading Teacher, 59*(7), 680–684.

Phillips, G., & McNaughton, S. (1990). The practice of storybook reading on preschoolers in mainstream New Zealand families. *Reading Research Quarterly, 25,* 196–212.

Ray, K. (1999). *Wondrous words: Writers and writing in the elementary classroom.* Urbana, IL: National Council of Teachers of English.

Ray, K. (2005). Read-aloud: Important teaching time. *School Talk, 10*(3), 1–3.

Reutzel, R., & Fawson, P. (2002). *Your classroom library: New ways to give it more teaching power.* New York: Scholastic.

Routman, R. (2003). *Reading essentials.* Portsmouth, NH: Heinemann.

Sibberson, F., & Szymusiak, K. (2003). *Still learning to read: Teaching students in grades 3–6.* Portland, ME: Stenhouse.

Sipe, L. (2000). The construction of literary understanding by first and second graders in oral response to picture storybook read-alouds. *Reading Research Quarterly, 35*(2), 252–275.

Sulzby, E. (1985). Children's emergent reading of favorite storybooks: A developmental study. *Reading Research Quarterly, 20*(4), 458–481.

Taylor, B., & Pearson, P. (2002). *Teaching reading: Effective schools, accomplished teachers.* Mahwah, NJ: Erlbaum.

Trelease, J. (1993). *Read all about it!* New York: Penguin.

Wasik, B., & Bond, M. (2001). Beyond the pages of a book: Interactive book reading and language development in preschool classrooms. *Journal of Educational Psychology, 93,* 243–250.

Wilhelm, J. (2001). *Improving comprehension with think-aloud strategies.* New York: Scholastic.

Williams, N., & Bauer, P. (2006). Pathways to affective accountability: Selecting, locating, and using children's books in elementary school classrooms. *The Reading Teacher, 60*(1), 14–22.

CHILDREN'S LITERATURE

Avi. (1985). *Bright shadow.* New York: Bradbury.

Carbone, E. (2006). *Blood on the river: Jamestown, 1607.* New York: Viking.

Crilley, M. (2001–2008). *Akiko pocket size* [Book series]. New York: Random House.

Curtis, P. (1999). *Bud, not Buddy.* New York: Delacorte.

Dahl, R. (1961). *James and the giant peach.* New York: Knopf.

Fritz, J. (1983). *The double life of Pocahontas.* New York: Putnam.

Fritz, J. (2007). *Who's saying what in Jamestown, Thomas Savage?* New York: Putnam.

Gownley, J. (n.d.). *Amelia rules!* [Book series]. Harrisburg, PA: Renaissance Press.

Hale, S. E. (2005). *Robert E. Lee: Duty and honor.* Peterborough, NH: Cobblestone .

Hotta, Y. (2005–2008). *Hikaru no go* [Book series]. San Francisco: VIZ Media.

Kurth, S. (2007–2008). *Graphic myths and legends.* Minneapolis, MN; Lerner.

Lange, K. (2007). *A new look at Jamestown.* Washington, DC: National Geographic.

Smith, J. (1992). *Bone* (Vol. 1). Worthington, OH: Cartoon Books.

Torres, J., & Bone, J. (n.d.). *Alison dare: Little Miss adventures.* Portland, OR: Oni Press.

Turner, A. (1992). *Katie's trunk.* New York: Macmillan.

White, E. B. (1952). *Charlotte's web.* New York: Harper.

Wisler, C. (1995). *Mr. Lincoln's drummer.* New York: Lodestar.

Woodruff, E. (1998). *Dear Austin.* New York: Knopf.

CHAPTER 4
GETTING TO KNOW YOUR STUDENTS

Just as the physical landscape of a classroom reflects a teacher's beliefs about how children learn, so do the types of classroom assessments a teacher utilizes. For example, on a particular day in Julie's classroom, after teaching a whole-group mini-lesson, the children disperse to various spots in the room to read independently, to write in their response journals, or to discuss their reading in dyads or small groups. Julie walks around with a clipboard and takes notes as she observes children engaged in literature discussions. Then she sits down on the floor by a child who is reading independently and starts to discuss the book while she jots down notes. She meets with several children individually, sometimes reading their response journals, and then calls a small group of children together in the back of the room to discuss the book they are reading together. Afterward, she makes notes about her observations of students' engagement and learning during the small-group lesson. Later, she reviews her notes, comparing them to previous notes she's made about individual students, and uses her cumulative knowledge of students' ongoing literacy development to inform her instruction during mini-lessons, to form and reform small groups, and to guide her thinking about individual student's literacy progress.

Ongoing informal assessment is an integral part of Julie's instructional activities. Julie uses assessment to:

➢ Observe students' responses to literature as they read independently and in small groups.

➢ Document various behaviors during individual students' reading and writing in response to reading.

➢ Evaluate students' progress in terms of past and present performances.

➢ Plan future instruction to meet students' individual and collective literacy needs.

FIGURE 4.1. Julie conducts an individual student reading conference.

Although this is a brief glimpse of one aspect of Julie's overall assessment practices, one can see how her perspective on assessment reflects her beliefs about children's literacy learning. While her school district requires many formal assessment measures, such as national and statewide standardized tests and benchmark tests, she finds that paying close attention to what students are doing when actively engaged in authentic reading and writing activities provides the most useful information for instructional decision making. This does not mean that Julie isn't accountable for standardized testing and grading. However, she believes that by providing effective instruction based on assessment *for* instruction, she can better prepare students for these challenges.

ASSESSMENT FOR ACCOUNTABILITY VERSUS ASSESSMENT FOR IMPROVED INSTRUCTION

As discussed in Chapter 2, annual standardized testing takes place in the fourth grade in the United States more than any other grade. The results are used to identify achievement trends for each school district, comparing them with state and national achievement levels. Some feel that this testing is necessary to guarantee continuous evaluation of student performance. Yet, standardized testing is costly, time consuming, and many question its value. Valencia, Hiebert, and Afflerbach (1994) state: "Standardized tests have not evolved with our research-based understanding of the reading process, and they are poorly aligned with classroom instruction that reflects this research and promotes the development of higher level thinking and complex literacies" (p. 7). Although standardized test results can be helpful in monitoring a school's overall effectiveness, the tests provide a limited view of readers' abilities and offer teachers little insight for effecting meaningful instruction (Neuman & Roskos, 1998). Winograd, Fores-Dueñas, and Arrington (2003) write:

> The most effective practices in literacy assessment are those that occur in the classroom between a competent teacher and a confident student. The most effective practices in literacy assessment occur when teachers and students work side by side in a trusting relationship that focuses on growth, nurturance, and self-evaluation. The problem we face, however, is nurturing these kinds of trusting relationships in a educational world dominated by the pressures to raise student achievement, as measured by high stakes accountability systems. (pp. 205–206)

Exemplary fourth-grade teachers prepare students for high-stakes testing through effective instruction that meets individual students' needs (Allington, 2002; Block & Mangieri, 2003). Alternative, authentic assessments can provide teachers with the information they need to make instructional decisions that move children forward in their literacy development.

PRINCIPLES OF EFFECTIVE CLASSROOM ASSESSMENT

Exemplary fourth-grade teachers spend many hours collecting and analyzing data from assessments in order to plan highly effective lessons targeted to meet students' exact needs (Block & Mangieri, 2003). Authentic classroom assessments provide insight into an individual student's attitude toward, and behaviors *during*, reading and writing. The information gained from individual assessments allows teachers to determine whether students are making progress in their literacy development. Authentic assessments:

➢ Are an integral part of informing and improving teaching.

➢ Help teachers discover what children know and can do.

➢ Have a specific purpose.

➢ Provide teachers with insights into each student's reading and writing processes.

➤ Help teachers identify each student's instructional needs.

➤ Are not so time consuming that they displace instruction.

Authentic assessments usually involve an informal, dynamic, and interactive process that takes place during natural experiences with text and carefully considers overall student growth in the reading/writing process. The following material provides examples of authentic classroom assessments for fourth-grade teachers. Figure 4.2 provides an overview of all of the assessments.

Anecdotal Notes

Observation is a powerful tool for assessment and evaluation. Much can be learned about students' reading, writing, and thinking by observing them as they engage in authentic literacy tasks. Most of the classroom activities in which students participate daily provide rich opportunities for observing students in the process of reading, writing, and thinking about texts. Anecdotal notes are one way teachers can document their observations. For example, in the opening of this chapter, Julie observed several children while they were engaged in independent reading, journal writing, and small-group discussions. The following notes are sample anecdotal notes:

10/24 John Book selection is too difficult. Needs help selecting . . .	10/24 LaKeisha Thoughtful discussion with Ann about their book. Asked ?'s, found . . .	10/24 Remi Used some word knowledge and spelling strategies when journal . . .

Observing approximately five students a day will ensure that all students are observed at least one time per week. Each week, alternate the activities observed to capture a multidimensional view of each student's literacy behavior. Documenting observations on sticky notes is helpful because the teacher can then easily place them in students' folders or portfolios for assessment and evaluation. Over time, anecdotal notes reveal a pattern of each student's ability to construct meaning.

Reading Interviews/Surveys

Students are motivated to read by different factors and engage in the reading process in different ways. Observations can assist teachers with understanding these differences, but some aspects of these factors and process can be revealed more saliently through interviews and surveys.

Reading interest inventories primarily provide information about individual students' interests and preferences for various reading materials. Information gleaned from students' responses to reading interest inventories, such as the example in Figure 4.3, can provide useful information for:

Assessment tool	Description of use	Suggestion for frequency of use
Anecdotal notes	Brief notes documenting observed behaviors whenever a child is engaged in reading and writing, including content subjects and group learning.	Throughout the year; select several students to observe and document each week.
Reading interviews/surveys	Used to understand students' habits, attitudes, book preferences, and behaviors when engaged in reading and writing processes.	Beginning, midyear, and end of the year to assess students' development over time.
Writing samples	The teacher or child selects a writing sample from the child's reading response journal or a piece of writing that reflects the writing process. If the child selects the sample, the teacher asks him or her to write reasons for why he or she selected this particular piece of writing. Analysis of the writing sample can assist the teacher in understanding a student's knowledge and use of strategies when writing.	Beginning, midyear, and end of the year to assess students' development over time.
Oral reading samples	Used to capture a student's observable reading behaviors, such as omissions, substitutions, insertions, repetitions, and self-corrections, when reading new or familiar text. Analysis of these behaviors can assist the teacher in understanding a student's knowledge and use of strategies when reading text.	Beginning-of-year baseline and ongoing.
Individual reading conferences	The teacher meets with a student one-on-one to discuss his or her reading. The conference may include book selection, text comprehension strategies, oral reading, and goal setting.	Beginning-of-year baseline; once every 1 or 2 weeks throughout the year, depending on student needs.

FIGURE 4.2. Overview of authentic assessments (*page 1 of 2*).

From *Teaching Literacy in Fourth Grade* by Denise Johnson. Copyright 2008 by The Guilford Press. Permission to photocopy this figure is granted to purchasers of this book for personal use only (see copyright page for details).

Assessment tool	Description of use	Suggestion for frequency of use
Reading and writing checklists	Serve as a quick reference for evaluating expected behaviors or strategies during students' reading and writing.	Beginning, midyear, and end of the year to assess students' development over time.
Reading logs	Used to provide a daily record of students' reading; time, genre, length, or other aspects of reading can be documented.	Ongoing
Reading response journals	Students write what they are thinking and learning about what they are reading. Analyses of their responses provide teachers with insight into a students' use of comprehension strategies when reading.	Ongoing
Retelling	Students retell orally or in writing what they have read. Analysis of retellings can clarify students' understanding of the sequence of events and their attention to the importance of story elements, details, and vocabulary.	Ongoing
Rubrics	A scoring tool that provides expectations for student performance on specific tasks. Criteria can be taken from standards set by the teacher, school, or district. Rubrics can be used to score response journals, writing, retelling, projects, or other activities. Students should be taught how to use rubrics to self-assess.	Ongoing; create and use as necessary.

FIGURE 4.2. (page 2 of 2)

1. Do you like to read?
2. How much time do you spend reading?
3. What books have you read lately?
4. Do you have a library card? How often do you use it?
5. What books have you checked out from the school library?
6. About how many books do you own?
7. What books would you like to own?
8. Put a checkmark next to the kind of reading you like best (topics you might like to read about):

_____History	_____Detective stories	_____Space
_____Travel/other countries	_____War stories	_____Humor
_____Plays	_____Poetry	_____Folktales
_____Sports	_____Cars/motorcycles	_____How-to books
_____Science fiction	_____Novels	_____Mysteries
_____Adventure	_____Biography	_____Art/drawing
_____Animals	_____Comics	_____Westerns
_____Graphic novels	_____Fantasy/magic	_____Computers

Other: _____

9. Do you like to read the newspaper?
10. If "yes," place a checkmark next to the part of the newspaper listed below you like to read.

_____Advertisements	_____Political stories
_____Entertainment	_____Current events
_____Columnists	_____Sports
_____Headlines	_____Editorials
_____Comic strips	_____Others: (please list)

11. Do you watch television? If so, what are your favorite television programs?
12. What is your favorite magazine?
13. Do you have a computer at home? If so, how much time do you spend using it?
14. What are your favorite websites or things you like to read on the computer?
15. Do you listen to audio books? If so, what audio book did you listen to most recently?
16. Do you have a favorite hobby or sport you play? If so, what is it?
17. What are the two best movies you have ever seen?
18. Who are your favorite entertainers and/or movie stars?
19. Do you enjoy having someone read aloud to you?
20. What does the word *reading* mean to you?

FIGURE 4.3. Sample reading interest inventory. From Hildebrant (2001, pp. 34–37). Copyright 2001. Adapted by permission.

> Stocking the classroom library.
> Selecting books for literature circles.
> Conferring with students about choosing books.
> Planning a home reading program.
> Selecting thematic units/topics across the curriculum.

Reading reflection surveys, such as the example in Figure 4.4, provide insight into how students perceive their own reading processes. A teacher's observation of a student's engagement in the reading process may confirm or conflict with a student's self-report. Information from the reading reflection survey can assist teachers with planning initial and ongoing instruction for:

Name: _____   Date: _____

How would you describe yourself as a reader?

What are you currently reading during independent reading time?

What are you going to read next?

What are you currently reading at home?

How do you choose the books you read?

What do you do when you get stuck on a word you don't know?

What do you do when you read something you don't understand?

What do you do when you start to read each day?

How do you keep track of the characters in the books you are reading?

What kind of reading is easy for you?

What kind of reading is hard for you?

FIGURE 4.4. Sample reading reflection survey. From Sibberson and Szymusiak (2003). Copyright 2003 by Stenhouse. Adapted by permission.

- ➢ Book selection
- ➢ Comprehension strategies
- ➢ Word-attack strategies
- ➢ Reading a variety of genres
- ➢ Strategies for sustaining reading when it become difficult or uninteresting
- ➢ Becoming aware of their own reading processes and setting goals for reading development over time

Reading interest inventories and reading reflection surveys can be given to the whole class, with students responding independently in writing or orally during individual reading conferences. Inventories can be given at the beginning, middle, and end of the year to provide ongoing information as students' interests and reading processes change over time.

Writing Samples

Reading and writing are reciprocal processes, meaning the development of one leads to the development of the other. A student's writing can provide a window to many aspects of his or her engagement with the reading process, such as understanding of text structure, story elements, author's purpose, use of details, and use of vocabulary. In this way, writing samples can be used to assess reading development. Of course, writing samples can also be used to assess the writing process by asking the following questions. Does the writing:

- ➢ Have a beginning, middle, and end?
- ➢ Follow a logical sequence for the writing genre selected?
- ➢ Stay on topic?
- ➢ Contain important details?
- ➢ Have varied and interesting sentences?
- ➢ Use correct grammar, punctuation, and spelling?

Rubrics can be used to assess criteria specific to writing a variety of fiction and nonfiction genres. Writing samples can be used to further teachers' understanding of a student's reading and writing processes and to inform instructional decisions based on an analysis of the writing samples. For example, if most writing samples reflect the need for instruction in the use of spelling strategies when writing, a teacher might determine to present one or more whole-class mini-lessons on the topic. On the other hand, if only a few students' writing samples reflect this need, the teacher may determine to provide instruction during individual conferences or small-group instruction.

Oral Reading Samples

Because the act of reading is a process, it is important to know how students process text to derive meaning. The best measure of students' ability to understand the texts they read with accuracy, ease, and fluency is to observe them while reading continuous text. However, fourth graders read silently, so in order to observe what is going on in their head while reading, we must observe them reading aloud. There are several ways to record students' oral reading in order to measure fluent processing and comprehension.

Informal Reading Inventories and Leveled Texts

An informal reading inventory provides samples of texts (fiction and nonfiction) in increasing difficulty or grade levels. Leveled texts can also be used for this purpose. Rather than leveled passages, leveled sets of books are used. The books are categorized along a continuum from easiest to hardest, according to the difficulty of processing demands. Several available leveling systems provide a gradient of text, such as the one by Fountas and Pinnell (2006), but it really doesn't matter which leveling system is used as long as it informs the teacher of the child's instructional level. The teacher should assess students' ability to read nonfiction texts as well as fiction texts. Just because a child can read and comprehend a piece of fiction at a specific level doesn't mean he or she is able to do the same with nonfiction (Stead, 2006). To support literacy learning across genres, teachers need to know how children attend to informational text structures and features such as a table of contents, glossary, index, graphic tables, maps, charts, and content vocabulary, in comparison to their ability to understand fiction.

Whether using passages from an informal reading inventory or a leveled set of books, students begin by silently reading a passage at grade level followed by reading the same passage orally. During oral reading, the teacher records the student's errors (see Figure 4.5 for one way to code oral reading errors). After reading the text orally, the student responds to comprehension questions or gives a retelling of the passage. Depending on the student's performance, he or she continues to more difficult or less difficult passages. To derive the accuracy rate (the number of words read correctly), count the errors and subtract the number from the total number of words in the passage. Accuracy is one indicator of the level of difficulty of a text for a particular student. Ninety percent accuracy or higher is considered good progress.

To determine the reading rate (fluency), time the reading and divide the number of words in the passage by the time it took to read it. A study by Pinnell and colleagues (1995) found that 64% of fourth-grade students read at 124 words per minute or slower; interestingly, students who read at 130 words per minute or higher had the highest average proficiency scores on the Integrated Reading Performance Oral Reading Fluency Scale (NAEP; see Figure 4.6). The scale can be used as a general guideline for determining students' reading fluency.

Behavior	Code	Counted as error
Accurate reading	✓ / text word	NA
Substitution	incorrect word / text word	Yes
Self-correction	incorrect word I SC / text word	No
Repetition	◄──────── R / text word(s)	No
Repetition with self-correction	incorrect word I R I SC / text word	No
Omission	− − / text word	Yes
Insertion	inserted word / − −	Yes
Long pause	# / text word	No
Told	text word I T	Yes

FIGURE 4.5. Coding reading behaviors.

From *Teaching Literacy in Fourth Grade* by Denise Johnson. Copyright 2008 by The Guilford Press. Permission to photocopy this figure is granted to purchasers of this book for personal use only (see copyright page for details).

From an analysis of students' oral reading patterns and responses to comprehension questions, teachers can get a picture of how they figure out unknown words in context, how they construct meaning, and their approximate level of reading. Many informal reading inventories are available on the market, but teachers can also create their own by using any gradient of text. Reproduce the text to have a copy to code while the child reads.

Running Records

Running records, developed by Marie Clay (1993), are another way to capture students' text-processing strategies through oral reading. Whereas informal reading inventories are a way to collect baseline data about students' text-processing strategies at the beginning of the year and again at mid- and end-of-year to document growth over time, running records provide a way to capture students' text-processing strategies throughout the year to inform ongoing instructional decisions.

Level 4	Reads primarily in large, meaningful phrase groups. Although some regressions, repetitions, and deviations from text may be present, these do not appear to detract from the overall structure of the story. Preservation of the author's syntax is consistent. Some or most of the story is read with expressive interpretation.
Level 3	Reads primarily in three- or four-word phrase groups. Some smaller groupings may be present. However, the majority of phrasing seems appropriate and preserves the syntax of the author. Little or no expressive interpretation is present.
Level 2	Reads primarily in two-word phrases with some three- or four-word groupings. Some word-by-word reading may be present. Word groupings may seem awkward and unrelated to larger context of sentences or passage.
Level 1	Reads primarily word by word. Occasional two-word or three-word phrases may occur—but these are infrequent and/or they do not preserve meaningful syntax.

FIGURE 4.6. NAEP's Integrated Reading Performance Record Oral Reading Fluency Scale. From Pinnell et al. (1995).

Running records can be taken during one-on-one conferences with the child on the text he or she is currently reading. The teacher sits beside the student and, using a blank sheet of paper and the coding system in Figure 4.5, records the student's reading of approximately 100 words from any point in the text. The oral reading can be followed up with a few comprehension questions or a retelling. The running record can be analyzed for accuracy and rate, as described above. The errors should also be analyzed to determine the kinds of information the student is using to process the text. Even very good readers make errors when reading. The difference is when the error(s) leads to lack of comprehension of the text. Analyze the errors to determine if they are:

➤ Semantically acceptable: The word makes sense in the context of the text.
   Child: *alignment*
   Text: The assignment did not seem particularly exciting to the student.

In this example, the child's substitution is not semantically acceptable because *alignment* alters the meaning of the sentence.

➤ Syntactically acceptable: The word fits grammatically in the sentence.
   Child: *didn't*
   Text: The assignment did not seem particularly exciting to the student.

In this example, the substituted word *didn't* for *did not* is syntactically acceptable because it fits grammatically in the sentence.

> Graphically similar: The word is visually or phonetically similar to the accurate word.
> *Child*:   *alignment*
> Text: The assignment did not seem particularly exciting to the student.

In this example, the substitution is visually similar because it begins and ends the same as the correct word (though it is not semantically or syntactically acceptable).

Based on the information gathered from analyzing running records over time, teachers can make more efficient decisions about instruction that will lead to greater comprehension of the text.

Individual Reading Conferences

Individual reading conferences provide a one-on-one, side-by-side opportunity for the teacher to observe a student reading real texts for real reasons and for the student to engage with the teacher in a real conversation about reading. Regie Routman (2003) writes: "And when students are assessed in connection with a book they are interested in—rather than a decontextualized test passage—optimal and accurate assessment is more likely. Also, the students do not view the conference as a test but more as a 'check-up,' a conversation" (p. 100).

The informal reading conference sheets in Figure 4.7 and 4.8 provide a sample of the type of information that can be gathered during a conference on fiction and nonfiction reading, including:

> Text selection—text difficulty, genre variety, sustained reading over time.

> Oral reading check—running record of approximately 100 words taken from any point where the student is currently reading.

> Comprehension check—a natural conversation following the running record and/or a retelling of the text.

> Goal setting—a discussion with the student regarding his or her reading strengths and goals for further reading development.

Reading and Writing Checklists

Checklists provide a list of observable characteristics related to reading, writing, listening, speaking, or viewing that can serve as a frame of reference to guide observations. Checklists can be used by the teacher as a way to become more knowledgeable about a student's strengths and needs in a particular area of learning. Checklists such as the example in Figure 4.9 can be used as a benchmark at

Name: _____ Date: _____

- Bring me a book that you can read pretty well.

Title of Book: _____ Genre: _____

- Why did you choose this book?

- What is the reading level of this book for you? ____ hard ____ easy
  ____ just right

- Tell me what the book is about so far.

- Read this part of the book for me. (Take notes as the child reads silently or orally.)

- Tell me what you remember about what you just read.

- Let's discuss your strengths and what you need to work on.
  Strengths:

  Goals:

- How long do you think it will take to complete this book?

FIGURE 4.7. Informal reading conference sheet. From Routman (2003). Copyright 2003 by Heinemann. Reprinted by permission.

the beginning, middle, and end of the year to record progress over time (numbers in the checklist in Figure 4.9 represent grading periods).

Reading Logs and Response Journals

Reading logs are affixed to the inside of the students' reading response journals and used to document the texts they read (see example below).

#	Title	Author	Genre	Date finished	Easy Just Right Hard
1	*Because of Winn-Dixie*	K. DiCamillo	RF	10/18	JR
2	*Gregor the Overlander*	S. Collins	F	11/2	JR
3	*The Snake Scientist*	S. Montgomery	NF	11/9	E

Reading behaviors _____
_____
_____
_____

Tell me about what you just read. _____
_____
_____
_____

If the student has difficulty getting started, use some of the following prompts:

What is the topic of the book?

How does the author present the information?

Why did the author write this?

What were some of the important points in the text?

What did you learn from reading this?

What did you learn about the topic that you did not already know?

Were there parts of the book that you did not understand? What questions do you still have?
What puzzled you? _____
_____
_____
_____

How did the author organize or arrange the text? Do you see a pattern or something the author
used over and over? _____
_____
_____
_____

Show me a place where you figured out a word because of clues the author gave you. _____
_____

What would you like to see the author add to this text? _____
_____
_____

What viewpoint does the author take on the topic? Is anyone else's opinion presented? _____
_____
_____

How long do you think it will take you to finish this text? _____

What subjects would you like to read about next? _____

How do you decide what to read about? _____
_____

FIGURE 4.8. Informal reading conference sheet for informational reading. From Hoyt, Mooney, and Parkes (2003). Copyright 2003 by Heinemann. Reprinted by permission.

Strategies	1	2	3	4	Comments
Predicting					
Sequencing					
Organizing					
Representation					
Identifying key ideas					
Refining/revising					
Drawing conclusions					
Comprehension	1	2	3	4	Comments
Recognizes story themes					
Recognizes purpose					
Synthesizes information across texts					
Expressive Abilities: Oral	1	2	3	4	Comments
Evaluates text using specific ideas					
Expresses ideas clearly					
Expressive Abilities: Written	1	2	3	4	Comments
Evaluates text using specific ideas					
Expresses ideas clearly					

Key: + Excellent   ✓ Satisfactory   — Needs Improvement

FIGURE 4.9. Language Skills Checklist. From Raphael, Pardo, and Highfield (2002). Copyright 2002 by Small Planet Communications, Inc. Reprinted by permission.

Reading logs or lists are a good way to assess the amount, type, and quality of a student's reading. Teachers can confer with students about their reading selections and set goals for expanding their reading repertoire.

Writing in response to literature can be an effective way for children to construct meaning from text. Students can use reading response journals to write their thinking about the texts they read. Figure 4.10 is an example of a student's reading response to *Artemis Fowl: The Artic Incident* written by Eoin Colfer (2001). This is the second book in the Artemis Fowl series about a 12-year-old evil genius who tries to restore his family fortune by capturing a fairy. Much can be learned about this student's engagement with the text by reading this journal entry. The student:

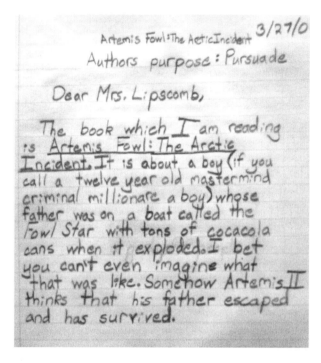

FIGURE 4.10. A writing sample from a fourth grader's reading journal.

> Recapped the story and summarized the plot.
> Understood the author's purpose.
> Connected with and elaborated on the main character
> Crafted a thoughtful, personal response to the text.
> Reflected on the reading and made interpretations and predictions based on his understanding of the text.
> Used interesting vocabulary to describe the characters and plot.
> Engaged in critical thinking about the text.

Based on the response, the teacher can engage in a meaningful conversation with the student about the book during conferences. Sometimes, teachers write a response in the journal, which can include questions or other comments that prompt the child to expand the breadth or depth of his or her thinking. Routman (2005) writes, "Many students, especially culturally and linguistically diverse students, substantially improve their writing—content, quantity, form, fluency—as a result of keeping these journals" (p. 125). It is important to establish guidelines for journal entries (see Figure 4.9) and to model and demonstrate for students many examples of journal entries over several weeks so that they understand what you expect.

Rubrics

A rubric is a performance-based scoring guide used to assess and evaluate the quality of a student's work against a predetermined set of criteria. It also articulates gradations of quality for each criterion, from excellent to poor. Therefore, rubrics focus on an expected learning outcome while representing a broad range of ability and serving as a guide for learning. Rubrics can be powerful tools for both teaching and assessment: "Rubrics can improve student performance as well as monitor it by making teachers' expectations clear and by showing students how to meet these expectations" (Goodrich, 1997, p. 14). To be effective, the design of a rubric is critical. For example, the two rubrics in Figures 4.11 and 4.12 present multidimensional criteria for literature response and informational report and describe varying degrees of quality from 5 (highest) on the left to 1 (lowest) on the right. These rubrics were created and published by the New Standards (2004) in connection with the performance standards for ELA discussed in Chapter 2 and designed specifically for fourth grade. They present a continuum of performance that allows teachers to identify similar performances from students in their classroom to see how far away from, or close to, standards they are. In their current form, they are too complex and abstract for use with children; rather they should serve as a template for guiding the development of appropriate classroom rubrics that address elements and strategies (p. 7).

For rubrics to be most effective, teachers should engage students in their creation. Goodrich (1997, pp. 15–16) recommends the following guidelines:

1. *Look at models.* Show students examples of good and not-so-good work. Identify the characteristics that make the good ones good and the bad ones bad.

2. *List criteria.* Use the discussion of models to begin a list of what counts in quality work.

3. *Articulate gradations of quality.* Describe the best and worst levels of quality, then fill in the middle levels based on your knowledge of common problems and the discussion of not-so-good work.

4. *Practice on models.* Have students use the rubrics to evaluate the models you gave them in the first step.

5. *Use self- and peer assessment.* Give students their assignment. As they work, stop them occasionally for self- and peer assessment.

6. *Revise.* Always give students time to revise their work based on the feedback they get in Step 5.

7. *Use teacher assessment.* Use the same rubric students used to assess their work yourself.

	5* Exceeds standard	4* Meets standard	3 Needs revision	2 Needs instruction	1 Needs substantial support
Orientation and context	• Introduces the topic. • Engages the reader and develops reader interest. • Conveys a knowledgeable stance.	• Introduces the topic. • Engages the reader and develops reader interest. • Conveys a knowledgeable stance.	• Introduces the topic. • May attempt to engage the reader.	• Introduces the topic. • May attempt to engage the reader.	• May simply refer to the book for an introduction. • Typically does not engage the reader.
Comprehension, interpretation, and evaluation of literature	• Demonstrates a comprehensive understanding of the work(s). • Focuses on the "big ideas" of the work(s). • Makes assertions about the meaning and/or quality of the work(s). • Presents interpretation and/or evaluation in a well-organized and coherent manner.	• Demonstrates a comprehensive understanding of the work(s). • Focuses on the "big ideas" of the work(s). • Makes assertions about the meaning and/or quality of the work(s). • Presents interpretation and/or evaluation in a well-organized and coherent manner.	• Demonstrates a literal understanding of the work(s). • May focus on the "big ideas" of the work(s). • May make assertions about the meaning or quality of the work(s) or parts of it. • May produce writing with some gaps in coherence.	• Demonstrates a literal or superficial understanding of portions of the work(s). • May make assertions about the meaning or quality of the work(s) or parts of it. • May produce writing that lacks coherence.	• Demonstrates some superficial understanding of portions of the work(s). • Rarely makes assertions about the meaning or quality of the work(s) or parts of it. • Typically produces writing that lacks coherence.

FIGURE 4.11. Elements of response to literature rubrics (*page 1 of 2*).

From *Teaching Literacy in Fourth Grade* by Denise Johnson. Copyright 2008 by The Guilford Press. Permission to photocopy this figure is granted to purchasers of this book for personal use only (see copyright page for details).

	5* Exceeds standard	4* Meets standard	3 Needs revision	2 Needs instruction	1 Needs substantial support
Evidence	• Summary, if present, provides enough detail so that the reader can understand the interpretation or the summary. • Provides adequate evidence from work to support interpretation or evaluation. • Quotations, if present, support interpretation or evaluation.	• Summary, if present, provides enough detail so that the reader can understand the interpretation or the summary. • Provides adequate evidence from work to support interpretation or evaluation. • Quotations, if present, support interpretation or evaluation.	• Summary, if present, may be incomplete or may focus on nonessential information. • May focus on random information or episodes in the work. • May rely on limited or inappropriate criteria to support interpretation or evaluation. • Quotations, if present, may support the interpretation or evaluation.	• Summary, if present, is incomplete or focuses on nonessential information. • May not use evidence from work to support evaluation or interpretation. • Typically does not use quotations. • If responding to an informational text, naming of the book's topic serves as "summary," and the focus is on facts in the text rather than the big ideas.	• Summary, if present, is scant or focuses on nonessential information. • Typically does not use evidence from work to support evaluation or interpretation. • Typically does not use quotations. • If responding to an informational text, naming of the book's topic serves as "summary," and the focus is on facts in the text rather than the big ideas.
Closure	• Provides closure.	• Provides closure.	• Provides closure.	• May provide closure.	• May provide closure.

*The criteria that define score points 4 and 5 are identical. This is intentional. What distinguishes a 5 from a 4 is not the presence or absence of a particular element or strategy. Rather, it is the overall quality of execution and the level of language the writer employs. Writers of score points papers bring something to the text that may not be provided by instruction—a deep understanding and/or passion for the topic and the genre.

FIGURE 4.11. (page 2 of 2)

	5 Exceeds standards	4 Meets standards	3 Needs revision	2 Needs instruction	1 Needs substantial support
Orientation and context	• Introduces the topic. • Engages the reader and develops reader interest. • Establishes context. • Conveys a knowledgeable stance.	• Introduces the topic. • Engages the reader and develops reader interest. • Establishes context. • Conveys a knowledgeable stance.	• Introduces the topic. • Engages the reader and develops reader interest. • May establish a context.	• Introduces the topic. • May attempt to engage the reader. • May attempt to establish a context.	• Introduces the topic. • Typically does not engage the reader. • Typically does not establish a context.
Organization of information	• Develops a controlling idea and/or a perspective on the subject (e.g., "Alligators are awesome"). • Creates an appropriate organizing structure.	• Develops a controlling idea and/or a perspective on the subject (e.g., "Alligators are awesome"). • Creates an appropriate organizing structure.	• Conveys a perspective on the subject. • May use a picture book format to organize information.	• Conveys a perspective on the subject. • May use a picture book format to organize information.	• May use a simple list structure or a picture book to organize information.
Development and specificity of information	• Reports well-developed and specific facts and information pertinent to the topic. • Communicates elaborated ideas, insights, or theories through facts, concrete details, quotations, statistics, or other information in support of the controlling idea or perspective.	• Reports well-developed and specific facts and information pertinent to the topic. • Communicates elaborated ideas, insights, or theories through facts, concrete details, quotations, statistics, or other information in support of the controlling idea or perspective.	• Reports on a topic but may lack adequate and/or specific facts and information pertinent to the topic.	• Reports on a topic but may lack adequate and/or specific facts and information pertinent to the topic.	• Reports on a topic but typically lacks adequate and/or specific facts and information pertinent to the topic.
Closure	• Provides a conclusion.	• Provides a conclusion.	• Provides a conclusion.	• May provide a conclusion or concluding statement.	• May provide a conclusion or concluding statement.

FIGURE 4.12. Elements of informational rubrics.

From *Teaching Literacy in Fourth Grade* by Denise Johnson. Copyright 2008 by The Guilford Press. Permission to photocopy this figure is granted to purchasers of this book for personal use only (see copyright page for details).

Give students a copy of the rubric so that they can engage in self- and peer assessment. Confer with students about their self-evaluations, giving them feedback on how it compares to yours. Of utmost importance is providing time for students to revise their work after reflection on self, peer, and teacher assessment. A major advantage of using rubrics for learning or assessment is that students develop skills for thinking about and reflecting on their learning that transfer to new learning situations.

Rubrics can also be used for grading. Work that reflects the highest level of quality for each criterion would earn an *A* and work that consistently falls in the lowest levels would earn a *D* or *F.* Since student work rarely falls in only one level of quality, many teachers average out the levels of quality.

GRADING FOR ACHIEVEMENT VERSUS GRADING FOR EFFORT

Teachers use *assessments* to gather information about students' learning. The process of judging that information to determine how well individual students are achieving or to make instructional decisions is *evaluation.* One prevalent type of assessment is giving students a test on information taught in class. If students achieve a certain score, it is assumed they have mastered the content. Yet, there are always students who somehow are able to pass the test but have not mastered the content, or students who cannot pass a test but clearly understand the content. Testing- or achievement-based grading doesn't provide the teacher with much information on which to base instructional decisions, especially for individual students, and it doesn't foster a learning environment in which all children believe effort counts. Allington (2002) writes: "Achievement-based grading—whereby the best performances get the best grades—operates to foster classrooms in which no one works very hard. The higher-achieving students don't have to put forth much effort to rank well, and the lower-achieving students soon realize that even working hard doesn't produce performances that compare well to those of higher-achieving students. If you are a lucky low achiever, hard work gets you a C in an achievement-based grading scheme" (p. 745).

A critical review of research on classroom assessment reveals that "the way to improve student achievement is not to do more testing . . . but rather to engage students deeply in the classroom assessment process and increase the specific, descriptive feedback they receive while they are learning" (Davies, 2004, p. 1). For example, teachers can create rubrics that define expectations for assignments or activities. With instruction, demonstration, and ongoing support, students can use rubrics as a guideline for completing assignments. One-on-one conferences provide feedback as to whether students are meeting the expectations outlined on the rubric. In this way, rubrics allow students to take responsibility for their own learning. Allington found that exemplary fourth-grade teachers evaluated student work and awarded grades based more on effort and improvement than simply on achievement. Thus, all students had a chance to earn good grades.

The school district in which Julie teaches does not begin formal grading (letter grades) until fourth grade. Thus, students and parents are anxious about receiving report cards with traditional letter grades for the first time. Julie explains:

> "Parents come to fourth grade concerned that their children are not ready for the academic transition of letter grades. My biggest concern for parents of fourth graders is their ability to look at the broader picture of helping their children to become lifelong learners. I want them to model the love of reading and talk with their children about books. I want them to find out what kind of books their children read and encourage that. A child needs to see that reading is lifelong and not just for school."

It is this perspective on literacy learning that guides Julie's thinking about the role of grading in classroom instruction. Julie focuses on her students' ongoing literacy development. She wants students to understand that she has high expectations for each of them, that she will support them in their learning, and with effort, they can achieve their literacy goals.

PULLING IT ALL TOGETHER: USING ASSESSMENT INFORMATION FOR EFFECTIVE INSTRUCTION

Collecting, organizing, and utilizing all of the information discussed in this chapter may seem overwhelming. Julie keeps a notebook with a divider for each child in the class. Each time she meets with a child individually or in a group, she places her sticky notes or observation sheets in the notebook with the appropriate child. Each day, she looks over the notes she has made in order plan for the next day's instruction. Julie knows that keeping track of her students' literacy development is important if she is to provide the appropriate support for their continued progress. For example, when asked to describe one child's progress based on the assessment data she has collected, Julie responded:

> "Matthew came in this year with high expectations for reading 'harder, longer' chapter books, and these expectations were reflected in his book selections early in the year. For example, one of the first books he selected was *Harry Potter V*. His mother had read the first four in the series to him, and he was excited about reading this one on his own. During my initial conferences with

him, we discussed the story and he shared his frustrations with figuring out the words and the overwhelming length of the book. I showed him how, as he read a section aloud, his fluency broke down, and I pointed out that he wasn't able to use strategies he "owned" to figure out unknown words and how this affected his comprehension of the story. I suggested that he make *Harry Potter V* a book he reads later in the year.

"From the reading attitude/interest interviews I gave at the beginning of the year, I was aware that many of my students were expecting to read 'hard, long' chapter books right off, and this showed up in their book selections. After conferencing with Matthew and several other students for whom selection of 'just right' books was a challenge, I revisited how to pick books in several subsequent whole-class mini-lessons. I helped Matthew select a book that didn't present such challenges for him. As we worked together over the year, his reading and writing became more analytical, and his vocabulary broadened. He is a 'thoughtful' reader now. He asks questions, makes personal connections, and has started paying attention to the author's purpose and writing style. These things are showing up in his writing, too. He is beginning to extend himself. Recently, he and a few other boys in the class started reading *Harry Potter V*. I think he is ready for it now. They read a few chapters and then meet to talk about it together. Matthew's participation and contributions to the group indicate that he is open to thinking about new ideas from others."

Julie reflected on her use of informal assessment data to make individual decisions for Matthew and the other children in her class. As with Julie, effective fourth-grade teachers evaluate student work more on improvement, progress, qualities, and effort than on the achievement of a singe standard (Allington & Johnston, 2002, p. 212). This chapter has described and provided examples of practical classroom assessment techniques to inform instructional decision making and meet individual students' needs. When making decisions about classroom assessment, consider the following points:

➢ Assessment should be aligned with how children learn and develop literacy.

➢ Assessment should determine what students know and can do.

➢ No one assessment technique can capture the multidimensional process of reading, writing, and thinking. Use multiple sources of information to create a broad picture of students' overall reading and writing behaviors.

➢ Use assessment techniques that capture the process of reading, such as running records, to examine students' text-processing strategies.

➢ Teach students to assess and reflect on their own progress by using rubrics and individual goal setting.

The information gathered from systematic, routine assessment, combined with knowledge of students' development as well as the process of reading and writing, will help teachers determine where students are in their literacy development and what they need to learn to move forward.

REFERENCES

Allington, R. (2002). What I've learned about effective reading instruction from a decade of studying exemplary elementary classroom teachers. *Phi Delta Kappan, 83*, 740–747.

Allington, R. L., & Johnston, P. H. (2002). *Reading to learn: Lessons from exemplary fourth-grade classrooms.* New York: Guilford Press.

Block, C. C., & Mangieri, J. N. (2003). *Exemplary literacy teachers: Promoting success for all children in grades K–5.* New York: Guilford Press.

Calkins, L. (2001). *The art of teaching reading.* Portsmouth, NH: Heinemann.

Clay, M. (1993). *An observation survey of early literacy achievement.* Portsmouth, NH: Heinemann.

Davies, A. (2004). Transforming learning and teaching through quality classroom assessment: What does the research say? In S. Frost & F. Sibberson (Eds.), *School Talk, 10*(1), 1–8.

Fountas, I., & Pinnell, G. (2006). *Leveled books K–8: Matching texts to readers for effective teaching.* Portsmouth, NH: Heinemann.

Goodrich, H. (1997). Understanding rubrics. *Educational Leadership, 54*(4), 14–17.

Hildebrant, D. (2001). But there's nothing good to read. *Media Spectrum: The Journal for Library Media Specialists in Michigan, 28*(3), 34–37.

Hoyt, L., Mooney, M., & Parkes, B. (2003). *Exploring informational text.* Portsmouth, NH: Heinemann.

Neuman, S., & Roskos, K. (1998). *Children achieving: Best practices in early literacy.* Newark, DE: International Reading Association.

New Standards. (2004). *Assessment for learning: Using rubrics to improve student writing (4th grade).* Pittsburgh, PA: National Center on Education and the Economy and the University of Pittsburgh.

Pinnell, G., Pikulski, J., Wixson, K., Campbell, J., Gough, P., & Beatty, A. (1995). *Listening to children read aloud: Data from NAEP's integrated reading performance record (IRPR) at grade 4* (Report No. 23-FR-04). Washington, DC: National Center for Education Statistics.

Raphael, T., Pardo, L., & Highfield, K. (2002). *Book club: A literature-based curriculum.* Lawrence, MA: Small Planet Communications.

Routman, R. (2003). *Reading essentials.* Portsmouth, NH: Heinemann.

Routman, R. (2005). *Writing essentials.* Portsmouth, NH: Heinemann.

Sibberson, F., & Szymusiak, K. (2003). *Still learning to read: Teaching students in grades 3–6.* Portland, ME: Stenhouse.

Stead, T. (2006). *Is that a fact?* Portsmouth, NH: Heinemann.

Valencia, S., Heibert, E., & Afflerbach, P. (1994). *Authentic reading assessment: Practices and possibilities.* Newark, DE: International Reading Association.

Winograd, P., Flores-Dueñas, L., & Arrington, H. (2003). Best practices in literacy assessment. In L. M. Morrow, L. B. Gambrell, & M. Pressley (Eds.), *Best practices in literacy instruction* (2nd ed., pp. 201–238). New York: Guilford Press.

CHILDREN'S LITERATURE

Colfer, E. (2001). *Artemis Fowl: The Arctic incident.* New York: Hyperion.
Rowling, J. K. (2003). *Harry Potter and the order of the phoenix.* New York: Arthur A. Levine Books.

CHAPTER 5

DIFFERENTIATING INSTRUCTION FOR DIVERSE LEARNERS

MEETING THE NEEDS OF DIVERSE LEARNERS

Classrooms across the country represent small microcosms of the population. According to the U.S. Census Bureau (2004):

➢ Forty percent of children under the age of 18 are members of cultural groups other than European American.

➢ Eighteen percent of children under the age of 18 live in homes where English is not the spoken language.

➢ Seventeen percent of children under the age of 18 live in poverty.

➢ Thirty-two percent of children under the age of 18 live with a single or adoptive parent or unrelated caregiver.

➢ Forty-seven percent of children under the age of 18 moved one or more times in the last 5 years.

➢ Six percent of children under the age of 18 have a physical or mental disability.

The term *diverse learners* refers to the differences in ability, interests, background knowledge, learning style, culture, and language that are represented in a classroom. Teachers face the challenge of how to work with a broad range of cultural, linguistic, and intellectual differences among their students. A recent longitudinal study by the National Center for Education Statistics (2006) followed

22,782 children from 944 schools across the United States from kindergarten through fifth grade from 1998 to 2004. The study collected descriptive statistics and test score data in the areas of reading, math, and science. Results indicated that children living in poverty scored lower than students at or above the poverty level. Students living in single-parent families were less likely to score in the top third than those in two-parent families. Students whose primary home language is English outperformed those whose home language was not English. African American students scored lower than students in other cultural groups. Boys scored higher than girls in the areas of math and science, and students who changed schools three or more times over the course of the study were less likely to score in the top third than students who moved two or fewer times.

Without successful intervention, many diverse learners are at risk of failure. How teachers address the varied needs of all their students and what they consider when planning and implementing literacy instruction are critical to the success of the diverse learners in their classrooms. This chapter outlines the following key elements of effective instruction that build on student diversity and promote effective learning:

➤ Focus on nonfiction.

➤ Plan instruction and group students flexibly to address their learning needs.

➤ Support student learning through teacher modeling, language, and scaffolded instruction.

➤ Use students' background knowledge and experiences as a springboard for literacy instruction.

➤ Explicitly teach nonfiction text structures.

➤ Engage students in using multiple comprehension strategies simultaneously.

➤ Assist students in making aesthetic connections to nonfiction.

➤ Provide opportunities for choice within the curriculum.

Focus on Nonfiction

Snow, Burns, and Griffin (1998) note that "reading difficulties may appear for the first time in fourth grade when the children are dealing more frequently, deeply, and widely with nonfiction materials in a variety of school subjects" (p. 78). Many students enter fourth grade having had little exposure to nonfiction and comprehension instruction in primary grades. Additionally, most of the content-area textbooks they will be required to read are poorly developed and written at a readability above a fourth-grade reading level. Roseman, Klum, and Shuttleworth (2003) state:

Today's textbooks cover too many topics without developing any of them well. Central concepts are not covered in enough depth to give students a chance to truly understand them. While many textbooks present the key ideas described in national and state standards document, few books help learn the ideas or help teachers teach them well.

In combination, the drawbacks inherent in textbooks and students' lack of prior knowledge and experience with nonfiction and comprehension strategies will leave many entering fourth graders unprepared and at risk for failure. In the real world, it is fair to say that most adults do not turn to textbooks for information on any subject, yet the majority of adult reading is nonfiction. When reading for information, most adults consult the newspaper, magazines, the Internet, and books on the topic. Using a textbook as a single source of information in the classroom not only limits the depth of information students learn about any subject, but does not prepare them for real-world reading.

As you have read throughout the chapters in this book, teachers can do much to meet the needs of all students in their classes, including diverse learners. The strategies discussed in this chapter focus on facilitating comprehension of a variety of nonfiction texts, because this type of comprehension is vital to students' success in and out of school.

Plan Instruction and Group Students Flexibly to Address Their Learning Needs

Over the past two decades grouping for instruction nearly disappeared, replaced with whole-class instruction. One reason for this shift is the plethora of research denouncing the prevalent practice of ability grouping. Groups designated by ability, usually according to standardized or criterion-referenced test scores, remain static throughout the year. Ability grouping has many negative effects for diverse learners, including the following:

➤ Students from minority groups are more likely to be assigned to low-ability groups.

➤ Students who did not have preschool experience are more likely to be assigned to low-ability groups.

➤ Students in low-ability groups receive lower-quality instruction and spend more time doing round-robin reading and workbook assignments than students in high-ability groups.

➤ Students in low-ability groups are more likely to exhibit inattentive behaviors than students in high-ability groups.

➤ Students in low-ability groups have lower academic expectations and suffer damage to self-esteem and social relationships.

➤ Teachers typically interrupt low-ability readers more often during oral reading when they miscue.

Due to these negative effects, many schools and teachers stopped small-group instruction all together, opting for only whole-class instruction. Though whole-class instruction certainly has its place in daily instruction, it should not be the only approach because those students who need more interaction and closer contact with the teacher and a text to be successful are marginalized.

Research has shown small-group instruction to be a critical component of effective instruction. Taylor, Pearson, Clark, and Walpole (2000) conducted a study of 70 first- through third-grade teachers from 14 low-income schools in four states and found that the teachers with high student achievement provided more small-group instruction. Allington and Johnston (2002) observed 30 fourth-grade teachers from five states and found that the most effective classrooms implemented small-group instruction.

As discussed in previous chapters, the reading workshop is an organizational structure that allows teachers to meet with students in whole-class, small-group, and individual settings during the language arts block. Through glimpses into Julie's classroom, you have seen multiple grouping scenarios. Julie reflects on her use of flexible grouping to meet student needs:

"I group students in many different ways, and my groups are always changing. Sometimes I group students by the subject of a book (perhaps a social studies novel), and at other times I group students who need to work on a specific skill, such as locating information or summarizing. Still other times I group students according to their choices. This helps them to be exposed to different personalities and dynamics. Most of all, I try to keep in mind what kinds of books will be most interesting and helpful and will increase their enjoyment of reading."

It is not simply the utilization of small groups that is the key to effective instruction in Julie's classroom. To meet the needs of diverse learners, she makes instructional decisions based on ongoing assessment and on the unique needs of each child in the classroom (see Figure 5.1 and Chapter 4).

Support Student Learning through Modeling, Language, and Scaffolded Instruction

Teachers foster comprehension development when they connect comprehension strategy instruction with in-depth learning of content in such disciplines as history and science. If students learn that these strategies are tools for understanding the ideas in texts, then the strategies become purposeful and integral to reading activities. Teachers can assist students in making these connections through modeling, language, and scaffolding.

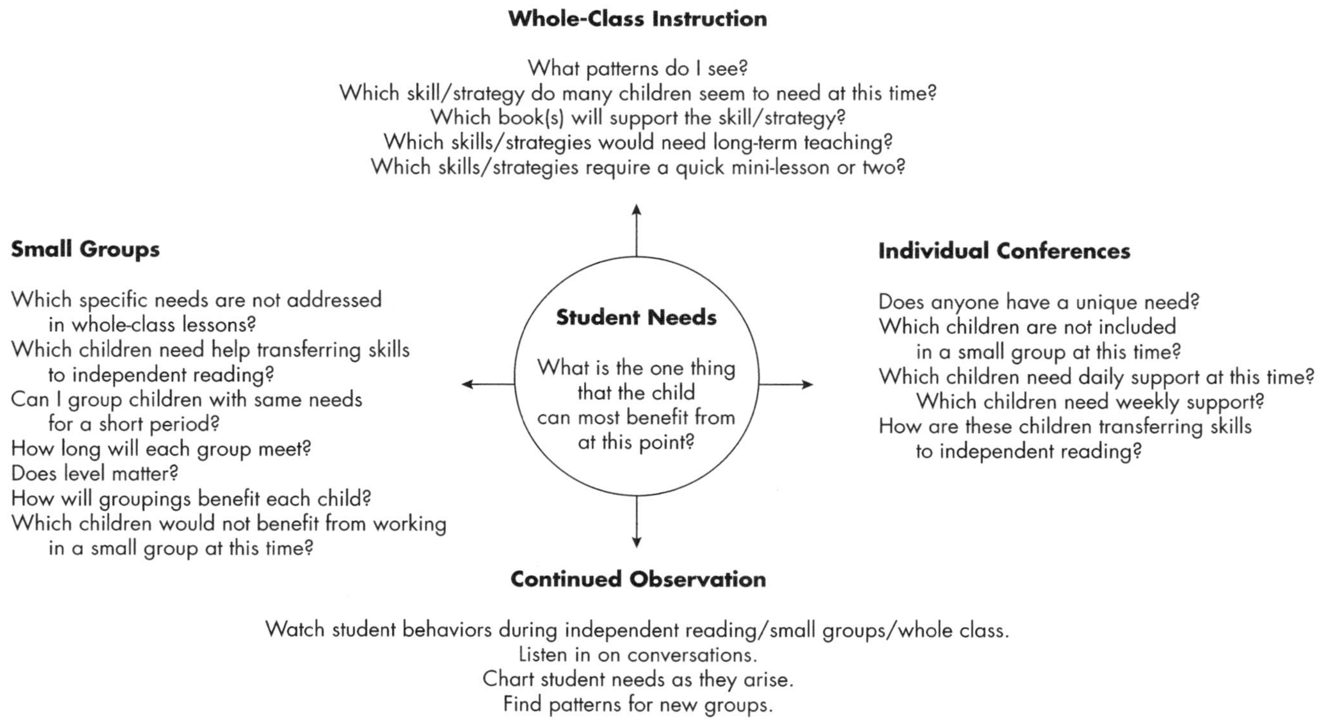

Whole-Class Instruction

What patterns do I see?
Which skill/strategy do many children seem to need at this time?
Which book(s) will support the skill/strategy?
Which skills/strategies would need long-term teaching?
Which skills/strategies require a quick mini-lesson or two?

Individual Conferences

Does anyone have a unique need?
Which children are not included
   in a small group at this time?
Which children need daily support at this time?
Which children need weekly support?
How are these children transferring skills
   to independent reading?

Student Needs

What is the one thing
that the child
can most benefit from
at this point?

Small Groups

Which specific needs are not addressed
   in whole-class lessons?
Which children need help transferring skills
   to independent reading?
Can I group children with same needs
   for a short period?
How long will each group meet?
Does level matter?
How will groupings benefit each child?
Which children would not benefit from working
   in a small group at this time?

Continued Observation

Watch student behaviors during independent reading/small groups/whole class.
Listen in on conversations.
Chart student needs as they arise.
Find patterns for new groups.

FIGURE 5.1. Grouping for instruction. From Sibberson and Szymusiak (2003). Copyright 2003 by Stenhouse. Reprinted by permission.

Nonfiction Read-Alouds

Reading aloud to children while modeling effective strategies for reading nonfiction text can familiarize children with the unique characteristics and conventions of expository text. When thinking about books to read aloud, nonfiction might not immediately come to mind, but teachers must make a conscientious choice to include nonfiction when reading aloud. The following are some guidelines for selecting and reading aloud nonfiction material:

➢ *Select only quality nonfiction.* Choose only those texts that meet the evaluation criteria of quality nonfiction books (see Figure 5.2). This ensures that books will be accurate; the information will be presented in an accessible, appealing, and interesting way; and the writing style will be engaging.

➢ *Select information from a variety of media.* When reading aloud from nonfiction sources, include newspapers, magazines, pamphlets, articles from the Internet, and brochures. Many times information from these sources connects with topics in the content-area curriculum and provides an authentic real-world connection to reading nonfiction for information.

Element	Criteria	Description
Organization	Is the book clearly organized in a way that shows the relationship between concepts? Does it organize the information in a way that aids in the understanding of the concepts?	There should be a clear pattern and sequence. Headings and subheadings can help organize the information. The organization needs to be logical and relate to the intended audience.
Style	Is the writing interesting? Does it show the author's enthusiasm for the topic? Does it draw the reader in by the use of language?	The information should be presented in a way that encourages the reader's involvement. The author's enthusiasm and relationship to the topic should be made evident by the tone of the work. A good work is precise with descriptive language.
Design and illustrations	Is the design visually appealing? Does it support and add to the content? Do the illustrations help solidify the reader's understanding of the topic?	The illustrations should relate to the topic on the given page and enhance the reader's understanding of the subject matter. Illustrations should be explained through captions or in the text. The format should be clear and appealing.
Accuracy, authority, and cultural authenticity	Is the information current and accurate? Is the author an expert on the topic? Does the information/illustrations authentically reflect the beliefs and values of the culture discussed?	The information needs to be up-to-date and verified by individuals in the field. The author should be qualified to write about the topic. Facts should support generalizations. Biases and stereotypes should be avoided.

FIGURE 5.2. Evaluation criteria for nonfiction information books. From Johnson (2008). Copyright 2008. Reprinted by permission.

➤ *Choose books that reflect children's interests.* Read nonfiction books aloud that reflect children's interests and that they recommend.

➤ *Consider reading only a portion of the book.* A nonfiction book does not necessarily have to be read from cover to cover. Read aloud a particular section of a book that you find interesting and model how to find that section by using the table of contents or the index.

➤ *Read aloud nonfiction with expression,* just as you would fiction. Make sure all children can see and hear and give them time to discuss the read-aloud along the way.

➤ *Discuss unfamiliar words.* Use unfamiliar or technical vocabulary as an opportunity to stop and think aloud about how to figure out unknown words. Encourage children to listen for interesting words or phrases in nonfiction.

➤ *Stop to discuss the organization and features.* Pause at appropriate times to discuss the organization of the text and identify special features and their purpose. Keep an anchor chart of what the children notice that can be revisited and added to over time (see Figure 5.3).

➤ *Reread favorite nonfiction titles* and make books read aloud available for children to read independently.

Think-Alouds

As discussed in the previous chapter, thinking aloud during reading aloud can make the invisible processes of reading visible. Think-alouds are particularly effective in showing students how to read nonfiction. How does a good reader figure out unknown words while reading nonfiction? How does a good reader make inferences between what the author states and what the reader knows when reading nonfiction? These are complex processes that take place in the head and can't be adequately taught through isolated skills. Julie states:

> "I use think-alouds to really talk about what I think while I'm reading. I show the students how to stop and reread because it doesn't make sense and model asking questions while I'm reading. I also model fluency, how to attack words I don't know, and how to discuss or write responses during conferences or journaling."

For example, when introducing the book *The Tarantula Scientist,* written by Sy Montgomery (2004), Julie used the following think-aloud:

➤ " *One of the good things readers do is* . . . use the title and cover illustrations to predict the content of a book.

➤ *From the title and cover illustration, I'm going to predict that* . . . this book is nonfiction because it looks like a photo of a real tarantula, and fiction books usually don't use real photos.

FIGURE 5.3. Anchor chart for understanding special features of nonfiction.

➤ *The photos help me to* . . . understand the many parts of a tarantula.

➤ *I'm connecting this to when* . . . I found a large spider in my house. It wasn't a tarantula, but I tried to figure out what kind of spider it was by looking at its size and color."

Other prompts include:

➤ "I'm thinking . . . "

➤ "I picturing in my mind . . . "

➤ "I don't understand this part so I'm going to go back and reread."

➤ "I'm connecting this part of the story to something that happened earlier in the story."

➤ "I think this character is . . . "

Once the process has been modeled for them numerous times, students can begin to conduct think-alouds on their own. Teachers can help children unlock the secret to nonfiction reading by lending their expertise to students through think-alouds.

Scaffold Student Learning

Scaffolding is a term used to describe the adjustments a teacher makes in her support of student learning, based on the constant feedback she receives during interactions with a child or children. During instruction, teachers assist and guide students to read, learn, and respond to text in ways they would not be able to do without support. Scaffolding is especially important when students are reading a challenging text or writing a difficult piece. At any point in time, teachers should scaffold instruction enough so that students do not give up on the task or fail at it, but not scaffold so much that students lose the opportunity to work actively on the problem themselves. Teachers continue to provide this support or scaffolding until students can read or write effectively on their own. This gradual withdrawal of instructional support is also known as a gradual release of responsibility: "supports" or "scaffolds" are gradually removed as students demonstrate greater degrees of proficiency.

Another important aspect of scaffolding is the teacher's use of language. In the classroom a teacher's language "creates realities and invites identities" (Johnston, 2004, p. 9). The way a teacher talks can position students in respect to what they are doing, learning, or studying. For instance, a teacher can *tell* a group of students to notice particular aspects of nonfiction text, in which case, students' attention is drawn to those aspects, which may be understood but not immediately used. On the other hand, if a teacher asks a group of students, "What did you notice?" the children become active in constructing their own knowledge. Johnston (2004) writes:

> No learner can afford to be dependent on the teacher for everything that needs to be noticed, so teachers have to teach children to look for possibilities. We draw children's attention to different patterns in text, words, and sounds, how print is different from illustrations, how it is laid out on the page, and so forth. We will also teach them ways of using these patterns when they notice them, but first they have to notice them. (p. 17)

Language such as the following opens the door for active thinking by positioning students as strategic learners in the classroom (Johnston, 2004):

➢ What kind of text is this?

➢ What have you learned most recently as a reader?

➢ How did you figure that out?

> ➤ How are you planning to go about this?
> ➤ Why?
> ➤ How else?
> ➤ What if?
> ➤ How did you know?
> ➤ Would you agree with that?

Anchor charts can be an effective scaffold for students' learning during instruction. Created by the teacher and children, anchor charts can highlight specific guidelines or behaviors for performing a particular literacy strategy, or they can serve as a concrete representation of students' thinking. For instance, after giving an explicit description of different components of a nonfiction books, the teacher could create an anchor chart documenting what the students noticed about nonfiction works (see Figures 5.4). Contents of the chart can be added to as children engage in reading the textbook independently. The anchor chart can be posted in a prominent place in the room to serve as a temporary scaffold for children's learning over time and can support children's understanding of the nonfiction genre.

Use Students' Background Knowledge and Experiences as a Springboard for Literacy Instruction

Many children entering fourth grade have limited prior knowledge of history or science. Limited or inaccurate prior knowledge interferes with students' compre-

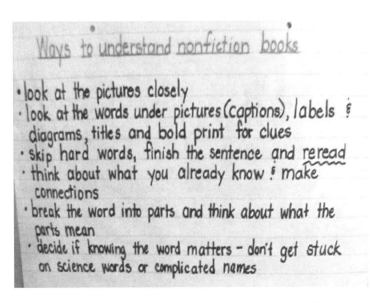

FIGURE 5.4. Anchor chart on understanding nonfiction.

hension. Therefore, one key aspect of understanding content information is the ability to access and build upon prior knowledge.

For example, research has shown that children's understanding of history is greatly enhanced when the context in which a historical event takes place is presented and discussed within a framework of other interrelated events. Picturebooks present pertinent historical information and illustrations in a brief yet complex and stimulating way that can be used to incrementally develop children's background knowledge of a particular historical event. Many picturebooks are available on the same historical event but from different contexts or perspectives. For example, slavery is a topic in the fourth-grade curriculum in Virginia. Julie builds students' background knowledge on slavery by reading aloud several historical fiction picture books:

➢ *White Socks Only* by Evelyn Coleman (1996). Grandma tells the story about her first trip alone into town during the days when segregation still existed in Mississippi.

➢ *Freedom Summer* by Deborah Wiles (2001). In 1964 Joe is pleased that a new law will allow his best friend, John Henry, who is "colored," to share the town pool and other public places with him, but he is dismayed to find that prejudice still exists.

➢ *The Other Side* by Jacqueline Woodson (2001). Two girls, one white and one black, gradually get to know each other as they sit on the fence that divides their town.

➢ *Rosa* by Nikki Giovanni (2005). The personal story of Rosa Parks's refusal to sit in the back of the bus, which leads to the Montgomery bus boycott and plays a pivotal role in catalyzing the Civil Rights Movement.

Another way to build background knowledge, facilitate accurate prediction making, and spark relevant question asking is by using the reading and analyzing nonfiction (RAN) strategy (Stead, 2006). The first step in the RAN strategy is a prereading activity in which the children brainstorm what they think they know about the topic under study and then post their ideas on the chart with sticky notes (see Figure 5.5). Asking children to respond to "what I think I know" "allows for approximations of knowledge" (Stead, 2006, p. 17). During reading, as the teacher and children read and research the topic, they either confirm their prior knowledge by moving sticky notes into column 2 or realize misconceptions by moving the notes into column 3. In this way, children compare and contrast information explicitly stated in the text or shown through illustrations. Children should be given the opportunity to discuss their thinking with partners, keeping each child focused and giving him or her time to talk. Column 4 encourages children to think about information that was not part of their prior knowledge but is new learning and constitutes much of the literal understandings of the text. Many times, this

What I think I know	Confirmed	Misconceptions	New information	Wonderings
Children state information they think is correct about the topic	Children research to confirm prior knowledge	Children research to discard prior knowledge	Children research to find additional information not stated in prior knowledge	Children raise questions based on the new information gathered

FIGURE 5.5. RAN strategy: reading and analyzing nonfiction strategies. From Stead (2006, p. 18). Copyright 2006 by Stenhouse. Reprinted by permission.

new information leads children to ask questions, which are then recorded in the fifth column, "Wonderings." Stead (2006) notes: "By encouraging children to make connections with prior knowledge I was also developing interpretive understandings. Evaluative understandings are also strengthened as children begin to question the validity of the information we are reading when it differs from other sources we have read in the past" (p. 19).

Explicitly Teach Nonfiction Text Structures

Students entering fourth grade may be familiar with how fiction or narrative texts work—characters in a certain setting experience events and seek resolution. Knowledge of how genres are structured allows children to anticipate what to expect and to make inferences based on those expectations; thus making reading easier.

Nonfiction texts are organized quite differently from other genres. There are five major organizational structures of nonfiction texts: description, problem–solution, chronological or sequential order, comparison–contrast, and cause–effect (see Figure 5.6). Knowledge of these core structures and signal words provides support to readers so that they can better anticipate language and features of each structure during reading and relate ideas to one another in ways that make them more understandable and more memorable. An effective way of helping students recognize and utilize nonfiction text structures is by using graphic organizers (see Figure 5.6).

Teachers can model how they analyze the text to figure out the structure and how knowing the structure can help with reading and understanding the information in the text.

Explicitly Teach Vocabulary

Research supports the fact that fourth graders with limited vocabularies are very likely to struggle to understand grade-level texts (Chall & Jacobs, 2003; National Institute of Child Health and Human Development, 2000; RAND Reading Study

Group, 2002). Low-income and English language learners, in particular, come to school with smaller vocabularies, and the gap only increases with time. Many activities for building vocabulary knowledge were presented in Chapter 2. However, no one strategy for learning words will work for all students. This section presents an additional strategy, the use of morphology, as another tool to put in students' toolkit for unlocking word meanings.

Morphology, the study of the structure of words or the breaking down of words (prefixes, root words, suffixes), has been found to be a strategy used most often by average and above-average word learners. A study by Kieffer and Lesaux (2007) found that fourth- and fifth-grade native speakers and English language learners in an urban setting with a greater understanding of morphology were more successful at learning academic vocabulary and comprehending text. They recommend four principles for teaching morphology to improve students' vocabulary and reading comprehension:

➤ *Principle 1.* Teach morphology in the context of rich, explicit vocabulary instruction.

➤ *Principle 2.* Teach students to use morphology as a cognitive strategy with explicit steps. Kieffer and Lesaux (2007) state that "using morphology to manipulate words is best understood as a cognitive strategy to be learned, not simply a set of rules to be memorized" (p. 140). They recommend following these four cognitive steps when breaking down a word:

    a. Recognize that he or she doesn't know the word or doesn't have a deep understanding of the meaning of the word.
    b. Analyze the word for morphemes he or she recognizes (both roots and suffixes). This process may be more difficult if the word is not transparent, particularly if it requires a change in both sound and spelling.
    c. Hypothesize a meaning for the word based on the word parts.
    d. Check the hypothesis against the context.

These four steps should be taught explicitly, modeled several times with various words, and students should be given time to practice them. In this way the teacher gradually releases responsibility for the process to the students.

➤ *Principle 3.* Teach the underlying morphological knowledge needed in two ways: both explicitly and in context. There are three types of knowledge of language students must know in order to use morphology effectively:

    a. *Knowledge of prefixes and suffixes* (see Table 5.1). Teachers can help students learn high-frequency prefixes and suffixes by providing a cumulative word wall on which these prefixes and suffixes are grouped by meaning and by allowing students to add new examples of word parts to the word wall from their own reading.
    b. *Knowledge of how words get transformed.* Students must understand the changes in sound and spelling that are often required to extract

Text pattern	Definition	Key words	Maps/webs	Examples of texts
Description	Descriptive details about characteristics, actions, or events	Descriptive adjectives and words such as *on, over, beyond, within*		*The Skeleton Inside You* by P. Balestino (1971) *Amazing Snakes* by A. Parsons (1990) *Bats* by G. Gibbons (1999)
Problem–solution	Set up a problem and its solution	*Propose, conclude, a solution, the reason for, the problem* or *question*		*A River Ran Wild* by L. Cherry (1992) *If You Traveled on the Underground Railroad* by E. Levine (1993)
Chronological–sequential	Give information in order of occurrence	*First, second, before, after, finally, then, next, earlier*		*Sugaring Time* by K. Lasky (1983) *The Buck Stops Here* by A. Provensen (1997) *Kennedy Assassinated! The World Morns* by W. Hampton (1997)

Comparison–contrast	Look at two or more items to establish similarities/differences	While, yet, but, rather, most, same, either, as well as, like, and unlike, as opposed to	Compare and Contrast with regard to Indicate which times are similar and which are different	*George vs. George* by R. Schanzer (2004) *Christmas in the Big House, Christmas in the Quarters* by P. McKissack (1994) *Talking Walls* by M. Knight (1992)
Cause–effect	Give a reason or explanation for a happening	Because, since, if–then, due to, as a result, for this reason, on account of, consequently	Effects Cause	*Girls Think of Everything: Stories of Ingenious Inventions by Women* by C. Thimmesh (2000) *A Drop of Water* by W. Wick (1997) *Sea Otter Rescue: The Aftermath of an Oil Spill* by R. Smith (1990)

FIGURE 5.6. Text structures in informational texts. Based on Hoyt, Mooney, and Parkes (2003) and Moss (2003).

TABLE 5.1. Most Common Prefixes and Suffixes in Order of Frequency

Highest frequency	High frequency	Medium frequency
	Prefixes	
un- (not, opposite of)	over- (too much)	trans- (across)
re- (again)	mis- (wrongly)	super- (above)
in-, im-, ir,- il- (not)	sub- (under)	semi- (half)
dis- (not, opposite of)	pre- (before)	anti- (against)
en-, em- (cause to)	inter- (between, among)	mid- (middle)
non- (not)		
under- (too little)		
in-, im- (in or into)		
	Suffixes	
-s (plurals)	-ly (characteristic of)	-al, ial (having characteristics of)
-ed (past tense)	-er, -or (person)	-y (characterized by)
-ing (present tense)	-ion, -tion (act, process)	-ness (state of, condition of)
	-ible, -able (can be done)	- ity, -ty (state of)
		-ic (having characteristic of)
		-ous, -eous, -ious (possessing the qualities of)
		-en (made of)
		-ive, -ative, itive (adjective form of a noun)
		-ful (full of)
		-less (without)

Note. From Kieffer and Lesaux (2007). Copyright 2007. Reprinted by permission.

roots from derived words (e.g., *strategy* [noun], *strategic* [adjective], *strategize* [verb], and *strategically* [adverb]). Teachers can create a word chart that displays these various forms of key words selected from the texts students are reading (Kieffer & Lesaux, 2007, p. 141).

c. *Knowledge of roots* (see Table 5.2). In order to understand new words by extracting roots from derived words, students must know the meaning of the roots. Teachers can teach some of the most common Latin and Greek roots, not by handing out a list to be memorized but by presenting the roots in a meaningful context at a time when they are most useful for students to comprehend a particular text (Kieffer & Lesaux, 2007, p. 141).

➤ *Principle 4.* For students with developed knowledge of Spanish, teach morphology in relation to cognate instruction. Working with Spanish-speaking students, Kieffer and Lesaux (2007) found that teaching cognates (i.e., words

TABLE 5.2. Common Latin and Greek Roots

Root	Definition	Example
	Common Latin roots	
audi	hear	audience, auditorium, audible, audition
dict	speak	dictate, predict, contradict, verdict, diction
port	carry	import, export, portable, porter, transport
rupt	break	abrupt, bankrupt, erupt, interrupt, rupture
scrib/script	write	describe, inscribe, prescribe, scribe
spect	see	inspect, respect, spectacles, spectator
struct	build	construct, destruct
tract	pull, drag	attract, detract, contract, subtract
vis	see	visible, supervise, vision, visionary
	Common Greek roots	
auto	self	automobile, automatic, autograph, autobiography
bio	life	biography, biology, biodegradable, biome
graph	written or drawn	graphic, telegraph, seismograph
hydro	water	dehydrate, hydrant, hydrodynamic
meter	measure	barometer, centimeter, diameter, thermometer
ology	study of	geology, biology, archeology
photo	light	photograph, photocopy, photosynthesis, photoelectric
scope	see	microscope, periscope, stethoscope, telescope
tele	distant	telephone, telescope, telecast, telegram

Note. From Kieffer and Lesaux (2007). Copyright 2007. Reprinted by permission.

with similar spelling and meaning in two languages) "has the potential to be a very powerful way for [these students] to use their first language as an asset to improve their English reading comprehension" (p. 142). They suggest that teachers subdivide their word wall into sections, including one for cognates, and encourage students to find them along with the common suffixes that are also cognates.

Provide Opportunities to Build Oral Reading Fluency

Fluency can be defined as "using smoothly integrated operations to process the meaning, language and print" (Fountas & Pinnell, 2006, p. 62). Evidence of oral reading fluency is found in students' ability to use phrasing (intonation, stress, pauses), syntax, or sentence structure (requires the reader to be aware of the ideas that are expressed in the text), expression, and accuracy when reading aloud. In order to read fluently, students must do the following (Fountas & Pinnell, 2006, p. 63):

➤ Process visual information rapidly.

➤ Understand how punctuation, pauses, pitch, and stress communicate the author's meaning.

➤ Read groups of words instead of single words.

➤ Use oral language and prior knowledge to anticipate what will happen next in the story.

➤ Notice dialogue and process it as the character's voice.

➤ Recognize features of known words to decipher words that are unknown.

➤ Rapidly access meaning.

➤ Not get bogged down in details.

Research indicates that fluency is highly correlated with comprehension (National Institute of Child Health and Human Development, 2000; Pinnell et al., 1995). The RAND Reading Study Group (2002) states: "We also know that language comprehension processes and higher-level processes affecting language comprehension (the application of world knowledge, reasoning, etc.) do not become fully operative in comprehending text until the child has acquired reasonable fluency" (p. 22). In Chapter 2, a study by Pinnell and colleagues (1995) was reported as finding that fourth graders who read with a higher rate of phrased and fluent reading scored higher on tests.

All students, but especially students who struggle with reading, need support to attain reading fluency. The following material describes ways in which teachers can provide students with opportunities for increasing fluency.

Prompting Fluency During Conferences

When you confer with students during individual reading conferences, you may prompt their oral reading in a way that increases their awareness of fluency. Some suggested prompts include the following (Fountas & Pinnell, 2001, p. 352):

➤ "How do you think your reading sounds?"

➤ "Read the punctuation."

➤ "Make your voice go down when you see the period."

➤ "Make your voice go up when you see the question mark."

➤ "Take a short breath when you see the comma [or dash]."

➤ "Use emphasis when you see the exclamation point."

➤ "Make it sound like the characters are talking."

➤ "Set off the parentheses by stopping before and after them."

➤ "Read it like this [model phrase unit]."

➢ "Put your words together so they sound like the way you talk."

➢ "Make your voice show what you think the author meant."

Buddy/Paired Reading

In buddy reading two students who read at similar levels read together. They can alternate pages, read in unison, or echo-read. Buddy reading can be an extension of a guided reading lesson or literature discussion group. In paired reading two students at different reading levels (selected by the teacher) sit side by side and read a text together. A more skilled reader is usually paired with a lower-level reader and provides support at points of difficulty, keeping the focus on fluency and comprehension (Dorn & Soffas, 2006).

Recorded Reading

In recorded reading a student listens to an audiobook on a CD or the Internet and reads aloud with the recording. LibriVox (*www.librivox.org*) is an online source that provides free audiobooks from the public domain. The children's catalog offers almost 60 titles, including *The Wind in the Willows* (Grahame, 1908), *The Secret Garden* (Burnett, 1911), and *The Wizard of Oz* (Baum, 1951).

Choral Reading

In choral reading individuals or groups of students read designated parts of a text. Some poetry books are specifically written for two or more voices. The Newbery-winning *Joyful Noise: Poems for Two Voices*, written by Paul Fleischman (1988), consists of 14 poems about insects. Students can be divided into two groups, each taking a side of the poem and reading alternatively until they have corresponding lines in which they read simultaneously. Choral reading can also be conducted in a cumulative style in which one student reads the first line and another student joins in reading the second line, picking up additional voices until the end of a stanza or the end of the poem. The reverse can also take place in which the whole class starts reading the poem together and then voices drop off until only one or a few remain at the end. A few more sources appropriate for fourth grade include:

➢ *I Am Phoenix: Poems for Two Voices* by Paul Fleischman (1985).

➢ *Big Talk: Poems for Four Voices* by Paul Fleischman (2000).

➢ *Math Talk: Mathematical Ideas in Poems for Two Voices* by Theoni Pappas (1993).

Choral reading allows children to experience the power of language, actively interpret a text, and increase oral fluency; indeed, it may be especially beneficial for English is a second language students. Hadaway, Vardell, and Young (2001) note: "For English L2 learners, teacher-guided choral reading of poetry meets many of the conditions that are critical in fostering oral language proficiency. Moreover, the focus on poetry is ideal when one considers the unique qualities of the genre: its brevity, strong rhythm, focused content, strong emotional connection, and powerful imagery" (p. 804).

Readers' Theatre

Readers' Theatre is an activity in which students read directly from scripts (no memorizing lines) mainly without props, costumes, or sets, although sometimes these are used. A part or all of a picturebook can be used for the script, and it may be modified to include more roles. Teachers can introduce children to this fun activity and then gradually turn over the responsibility to the students for writing the script, assigning parts, obtaining props if desired, and performing for each other. Children are encouraged to read with expression and use gestures appropriate for their character. This activity encourages a deeper insight into the character and an understanding of the story as well as increasing fluency.

Readers' Theatre scripts are available from publishers or can be easily created from picturebooks and chapter books. The following are a few examples:

➢ *Wham! It's a Poetry Jam: Discovering Performance Poetry* by Sara Holbrook (2002). Contains over 30 poems along with tips on how to perform them.

➢ *Sleeping Ugly* by Jane Yolen (1981). When beautiful Princess Miserella, Plain Jane, and a fairy fall under a sleeping spell, a prince undoes the spell in a surprising way. This fractured fairytale can be easily adapted for Readers' Theatre.

➢ *The Great Kapok Tree* by Lynne Cherry (1990). The many different animals that live in a great kapok tree in the Brazilian rainforest try to convince a man with an ax of the importance of not cutting down their home. This story can be easily adapted for choral reading or Readers' Theatre.

Engage Students in Using Multiple Comprehension Strategies Simultaneously

In Chapter 2, seven comprehension strategies were presented that have been found to be effective in improving students' comprehension of text: making connections, monitoring reading, determining importance, visualizing, making inferences, synthesizing, and questioning. Students must learn to use these strategies simultaneously as they read.

For example, inferring requires the reader to use stated facts in the text, make connections to prior knowledge and experiences, and draw conclusions beyond the text. For example, the picturebook *Encounter* by Jane Yolen (1992) is written from the point of view of a Taino Indian boy on the island of San Salvador as he witnesses the landing of Columbus and his men in 1492. When Columbus and his men come on to the shore, the young boy is afraid. The boy observes three of

Columbus's men "push sticks into the sand." From the illustration accompanying the text, the reader can see that the sticks support the Spanish flag. The young boy remarks, "Then I was even more afraid." The reader must infer from the text and the illustration why raising the flag would make the boy afraid. One might make a connection to prior knowledge of the first landing on the moon or the Olympics in which a person has proudly accomplished a great feat and claims the victory for their country. One might then draw the conclusion that the boy's instinct warned him that such events by strangers would be an act of staking a claim or taking ownership and this would cause him to be afraid for himself and his people. This text-to-world inference requires the reader to understand the literal facts and then connect those facts to prior knowledge.

Teachers must provide continual support for diverse learners in their use of multiple strategies. Questioning the author (QtA; Beck, McKeown, Hamilton, & Kucan, 1997) is a technique in which the teacher supports students' interactions with the text by intervening at selected points and asking guiding queries. The following queries can be useful in addressing nonfiction text:

Initiating queries

➢ "What is the author trying to say here?"

➢ "What is the author's message?"

➢ "Why is the author telling us that?"

Follow-up queries

➢ "What does the author mean here?"

➢ "Does the author explain this clearly?"

➢ "How could the author have said things more clearly?"

➢ "What would you say instead?"

Julie used the QtA when starting a new chapter in the social studies textbook on slavery in Virginia (see Figure 5.7). The opening page of the chapter titled "The Issue of Slavery" begins with the following journal entry:

November 1824

We arrived at Montpelier, the home of James Madison, late yesterday. It is a beautiful home in beautiful country. I am grateful that our visit here will last four days. Traveling with the Marquis de Lafayette on this tour of the United States has tired me. Today we looked around the large property. Lafayette is most interested in visiting Mr. Madison's workers—slaves. He cannot understand how a country so in love with freedom can allow slavery. I have overheard Lafayette say to his old friend, "All men without exception have a right to liberty." (Scott Foresman, 2003, p. 268)

FIGURE 5.7. Julie conducts a small-group mini-lesson in which she models how to read the social studies textbook.

There is no indication as to who wrote the entry and no connection between the entry and the next section of text in the book. After reading the entry aloud, Julie asked, "What is the author trying to say in this journal entry?" One of the students replied, "That slavery is wrong." Julie followed up the student's response by asking the class, "What gives her [the student] that idea?" Another student responded, "Because it says Lafayette doesn't understand why there's slavery when we love freedom so much." Julie agreed with the student's comment, "I think you are both right—Lafayette thinks slavery is wrong because all people have the right to freedom."

Now that Julie has helped the students understand the purpose of the journal entry, she asked, "Why do you think the author is telling us what Lafayette thinks about slavery in Virginia?" After a few minutes, one student replied, "Maybe because Lafayette is an important person." Another student quickly added, "Yeah, I remember we learned about him when we studied the Revolution. He's from France and helped us win." Julie restated the students' thoughts and asked a follow-up question: "So, the author is telling us Lafayette's thoughts because he is someone whose opinion America values. But why do you think the author is giving us Lafayette's thoughts at the very beginning of the chapter?" A student commented, "So we know that even though we had slavery in Virginia, important people like Lafayette, who helped us get our freedom, didn't think it was right."

Through this exchange, the students were led to a deeper understanding of the implied message in the text. QtA provides students with a set of useful thinking strategies for all genres, but can be especially helpful with textbook reading, because the queries and discussion can help children understand that textbooks don't provide the depth of information necessary to fully understand the concept. Allington (2006) writes: "QtA is a powerful strategy for helping struggling readers not only better understand the texts they read, but also understand that some texts are just hard to understand for any number of reasons. This 'blame the author' feature—she just didn't write it very clearly—can be empowering for struggling readers" (p. 135).

When planning a QtA lesson, teachers should keep in mind three major goals (Allington, 2006, p. 74):

1. Identify the major understandings students should construct and anticipate potential problems in the text.

2. Segment the text to focus on information needed to build understandings.

3. Develop queries that promote the building of those understandings.

QtA also provides a scaffold for children's independent book discussions, which are discussed in the next section.

Another way to engage children in using multiple comprehension strategies is by pairing nonfiction and fiction books on the same topic. Giles and Pierce (2001) write: "Juxtaposing fiction and nonfiction builds on the natural curiosity of students. The fictional accounts draw readers into the story world while the nonfiction texts add facts and depth to students' understanding" (p. 578). For example, in the fiction book *Just a Dream,* written and illustrated by Chris Van Allsburg (1990), a young boy named Walter has a dream about a future Earth devastated by pollution and begins to understand the importance of taking care of the environment. The book's environmental message is clear: Don't pollute. However, the book does not explain the causes of the Earth's different pollutions or what can be done to protect it. Students can be encouraged to think about their own knowledge regarding sources of pollutants. Drawing on students' implicit understandings, *Just a Dream* can be paired with a nonfiction text such as *Global Pollution,* written by Paul Brown (2003), to provide accurate information about pollutants, including ways people can help:

Buy recycled products whenever you can. By buying them you help to create a market demand for them, which will encourage more recycling. Consolidate all your shopping into one or two bags, instead of getting a new one at every store. You can even take your own shopping bag with you when you shop. Waste caused by plastic bags is a major problem all around the world. (p. 48)

Students can be prompted to use the explicit information in the texts and implicit understandings from their background knowledge and experiences to make judgments about whether these efforts will result in removal of various forms of pollutants from the Earth.

Assist Students in Making Aesthetic Connections to Nonfiction Texts

Most people read nonfiction with an efferent stance; that is, with the expectation that they are going to learn something. Yet, it is the aesthetic or emotional response to what we read that makes the information meaningful. Typically, a strong emotional response is associated with the well-developed characters and plot lines of fiction. However, we do sometimes react emotionally to nonfiction. In the now classic *Independence in Reading* (1980), Don Holdaway asserts: "It is difficult to provide natural motivation for reading in an environment where books are things you work through rather than things you come to depend on for special pleasure and enlightenment" (p. 25). A nonfiction book has the potential to magnify and enhance the reader's personal interaction with a subject. Teachers can supplement textbooks with nonfiction trade books that can elicit motivation, enthusiasm, caring, and insight into just about any aspect of the curriculum, inspiring children to do their own research or further reading to learn more. Stead (2006) states: "Even though it is important for readers to be able to recall facts and locate new information, it is when they connect with the information they read that even deeper meaning occurs" (p. 90). Engaging students in writing responses and participating in discussions about nonfiction text can assist them in making aesthetic connections.

Journal Responses

The previous chapters discussed using reading response journals to involve students in responding to fiction texts. Students can also respond to informational texts. Two-column journals are a way for students to record both aesthetic and efferent responses to a text. The first column can be used to copy or paraphrase information from the text that the student finds interesting, and the other column is for the student to write his or her thoughts or feelings about that information, as illustrated in Figure 5.8.

Teachers should model how to write two-column journal entries many times to scaffold expectations and students' understanding of the process.

Information from the text	Student's thoughts/feelings
The head of a pin can hold 300 trillion water molecules.	That is so hard to believe—the photo helped me.
Adding soap to water weakens the surface tension and allows the water to stretch without breaking.	We learned about this when we studied surface tension and made bubbles and wrote poems about them.
In this photography, we can see how water reflects and bends light.	I don't understand what it means by bending light.

FIGURE 5.8. Two-column journal on *A Drop of Water* by Walter Wick (1997).

Literature Discussions

Allington's (2006) review of several research studies indicated that "in the typical classroom the assigned tasks overwhelmingly emphasize copying, remembering, and reciting, with few tasks assigned that engaged students in discussions about what they've read" (p. 117). Yet, research supports the fact that opportunities to engage in discussion about texts are related to improved student achievement (Allington, 2006). In fact, students in exemplary teachers' classrooms are more likely to be engaged in peer conversations about texts.

Content-area literature circles provide students with the opportunity to decide what to discuss, based on their own interests, and therefore are a motivating and authentic context for diverse learners. However, students may be unfamiliar with literature circles in general or with participating in literature circles about expository text. Students will need a high level of teacher support in the beginning (see guidelines for facilitating literature circles in Chapter 3, pp. 61–64).

Several activities previously discussed in this chapter can serve as springboards to literature discussions about nonfiction texts. The RAN strategy can elicit questions students have about nonfiction texts they want to discuss. The QtA strategy can also provide a framework for discussing nonfiction. In addition, sticky notes from students' think-alouds and journal responses can spark questions.

Provide Opportunities for Choice within the Curriculum

Most fourth graders are truly interested in many of the topics studied in school and, if given the chance, will engage in further reading and writing about these texts independently. Engagement in reading for authentic purposes results in increased motivation, comprehension, and strategic reading.

This chapter provided organizational structures and strategies for meeting the needs of diverse learners in the fourth-grade classroom. Without receiving specific, explicit instruction and ongoing supports across and within a range of literacy contexts and genres, especially content-area nonfiction, these students will be at risk of failure. The next chapter describes how Julie sets up her classroom and structures her daily routines and schedule to organize instruction in a way that meets all students' needs.

REFERENCES

Allington, R. L. (2006). *What really matters for struggling readers* (2nd ed.). Boston: Pearson/Allyn & Bacon.

Allington, R. L., & Johnston, P. N. (2002). *Reading to learn: Lessons from exemplary fourth-grade classrooms.* New York: Guilford Press.

Beck, I., McKeown, M., Hamilton, R., & Kucan, L. (1997). *Questioning the author: An approach to enhancing student engagement with text.* Newark, DE: International Reading Association.

Chall, J., & Jacobs, V. (2003). Poor children's fourth-grade slump. *American Educator, 27*(1), 14–15, 44.

Dorn, L., & Soffas, C. (2006). *Teaching for deep comprehension.* Portland, ME: Stenhouse.

Duke, N. (2004). The case for informational text. *Educational Leadership, 61*(6), 40–44.

Fountas, I., & Pinnell, G. (2001). *Guiding readers and writers grades 3–6: Teaching comprehension, genre, and content literacy.* Portsmouth, NH: Heinemann.

Fountas, I., & Pinnell, G. (2006). *Teaching for comprehension and fluency.* Portsmouth, NH: Heinemann.

Giles, C., & Pierce, K. (2001). Pairing fact and fiction for deep understanding. *Language Arts, 78*(6), 579–588.

Hadaway, N., Vardell, S., & Young, T. (2001). Scaffolding oral language development through poetry for students learning English. *The Reading Teacher, 54,* 796–806.

Holbrook, S. (2002). *Wham! It's a poetry jam: Discovering performance poetry.* Homesdale, PA: Boyds Mills Press.

Holdaway, D. (1980). *Independence in reading.* New York: Scholastic.

Hoyt, L., Mooney, M., & Parkes, B. (2003). *Exploring informational texts.* Portsmouth, NH: Heinemann.

Johnson, D. (2008). *The joy of children's literature.* Boston: Houghton Mifflin.

Johnston, P. (2004). *Choice words: How our language affects children's learning.* Portland, ME: Stenhouse.

Kieffer, M., & Lesaux, N. (2007). Breaking down words to build meaning: Morphology, vocabulary, and reading comprehension in the urban classroom. *The Reading Teacher, 61*(2), 134–144.

National Center for Education Statistics. (2006). *Characteristics of schools, districts, teachers, principals, and school libraries in the United States: 2003–04 schools and staffing survey.* Washington, DC: Author. Retrieved March 25, 2006, from *www.nces.ed.gov/pubs2006/2006313.pdf*

National Institute for Child Health and Human Development. (2000). *Report of the National Reading Panel: Teaching children to read: An evidence-based assessment of the scientific research literature on reading and its implications for reading instruction: Report of the subgroup* (NIH Pub. No. 00-4754). Washington, DC: U.S. Department of Health and Human Services.

Pinnell, G., Pikulski, J., Wixson, K., Campbell, J., Gough, P., & Beatty, A. (1995). *Listening to children read aloud: Oral fluency.* Washington, DC: U.S. Department of Education, National Center for Educational Statistics. Retrieved February 20, 2006, from *www.nces.ed.gov/pubs95/web/95762.asp*

RAND Study Group. (2002). *Reading for understanding: Toward an R&D program in reading comprehension.* Arlington, VA: RAND Corporation.

Roseman, J., Kulm, G., & Shuttleworth, S. (2003). *Putting textbooks to the test.* Washington, DC: Project 2061, American Association for the Advancement of Science. Retrieved May 20, 2005, from *www.project2061.org/research/articles/enc.htm*

Scott Foresman. (2003). *Social studies: Virginia.* Upper Saddle River, NJ: Pearson Education.

Sibberson, F., & Szymusiak, K. (2003). *Still learning to read: Teaching students in grades 3–6.* Portland, ME: Stenhouse.

Snow, C., Burns, S., & Griffin, P. (1998). *Preventing reading difficulties in young children.* Washington, DC: National Academy Press.

Stead, T. (2006). *Reality checks: Teaching reading comprehension with nonfiction K–5.* Portland, ME: Stenhouse.

Taylor, B., Pearson, P. D., Clark, K., & Walpole, S. (2000). Effective schools and accomplished teachers: Lessons about primary grade reading instruction in low-income schools. *Elementary School Journal, 101*(2), 121–166.

U.S. Census Bureau. (2004, March). *Children and the households they live in: 2000.* Washington, DC: Author. Retrieved March 25, 2006, from *www.census.gov/prod/2004pubs/censr-14.pdf*

Wilhelm, J. (2001). *Improving comprehension with think-aloud strategies.* New York: Scholastic.

CHILDREN'S LITERATURE

Balestino, P. (1971). *The skeleton inside you.* New York: Crowell.

Baum, F. (1951). *The wizard of Oz.* New York: Wonder Books.

Brown, P. (2003). *Global pollution.* Portsmouth, NH: Heinemann.

Burnett, F. (1911). *The secret garden.* New York: Frederick A. Stokes.

Cherry, L. (1990). *The great kapok tree.* New York: Harcourt.

Cherry, L. (1992). *A river ran wild.* San Diego, CA: Harcourt, Brace, Jovanovich.

Coleman, E. (1996). *White socks only.* Morton Grove, IL: Whitman.

Fleischman, P. (1985). *I am Phoenix: Poems for two voices.* New York: HarperCollins.

Fleischman, P. (1988). *Joyful noise: Poems for two voices.* New York: Harper & Row.

Fleischman, P. (2000). *Big talk: Poems for four voices.* Cambridge, MA: Candlewick Press.

Gibbons, G. (1999). *Bats.* New York: Holiday House.

Giovanni, N. (2005). *Rosa.* New York: Holt.

Grahame, K. (1908). *The wind in the willows.* New York: Charles Scribner's Sons.

Hampton, W. (1997). *Kennedy assassinated: The world mourns.* Cambridge, MA: Candlewick.

Knight, M. (1992). *Talking walls.* Gardiner, ME: Tilbury House.

Lasky, K. (1983). *Sugaring time.* New York: Macmillan.

Levine, E. (1993). *If you traveled on the Underground Railroad.* New York: Scholastic.

McKissack, P. (1994). *Christmas in the big house, Christmas in the quarters.* New York: Scholastic.

Montgomery, S. (2004). *The tarantula scientist.* Boston: Houghton Mifflin.

Pappas, T. (1993). *Math talk: Mathematical ideas in poems for two voices.* San Carlos, CA: World Wide.

Parsons, A. (1990). *Amazing snakes*. New York: Knopf.

Provensen, A. (1997). *The buck stops here*. San Diego, CA: Browndeer Press.

Schanzer, R. (2004). *George vs. George*. Washington, DC: National Geographic.

Smith, R. (1990). *Sea otter rescue: The aftermath of an oil spill*. New York: Cobblehill Books.

Thimmesh, C. (2000). *Girls think of everything: Stories of ingenious inventions by women*. Boston: Houghton Mifflin.

Van Allsburg, C. (1990). *Just a dream*. Boston: Houghton Mifflin.

Wick, W. (1997). *A drop of water*. New York: Scholastic.

Wiles, D. (2001). *Freedom summer*. New York: Atheneum.

Woodson, J. (2001). *The other side*. New York: Putnam.

Yolen, J. (1992). *Encounter*. New York: Harcourt.

Yolen, J. (1981). *Sleeping ugly*. New York: Coward, McCann & Geoghegan.

CHAPTER 6

A WEEK IN A FOURTH-GRADE CLASSROOM

T he previous chapters have described the research-based instructional practices (to review, look at the section at the end of Chapter 2, "What We Know about Effective Fourth-Grade Teachers"). You were introduced to Julie, a highly effective fourth-grade teacher, and glimpsed her use of effective practices through descriptions of her teaching and samples of her students' work. In this chapter, you have the opportunity to see how all of the components discussed separately in the previous chapters come together in the context of typical day in fourth grade.

ESTABLISHING ROUTINES

By fourth grade students understand the expectations of classroom life: Raise your hand to ask a question, line up quietly when leaving the classroom, keep your hands and feet to yourself at all times, and so on. But, every teacher has his or her own way of doing things. It is important to take time at the beginning of the year to establish routines. Ensuring that students understand and follow classroom routines from the start fosters independence and optimal learning the rest of the school year.

Mini-lessons can be used to present procedural routines such as going to the bathroom, asking questions, and where to get materials. Julie states: "If you expect the classroom to run in an organized manner, you have to be sure to keep things readily accessible to the students. All materials to be borrowed, such as dictionaries, extra glue, and paper, are kept in a spot the students can easily get to without distracting others. They don't ask permission, they know that these things are for sharing and to return them for others to share."

125

Mini-lessons are also great for introducing instructional routines such as a reading/writing workshop. Julie relates:

"I truly believe if you expect kids to be so independent, you have to provide them with your expectations of a structured environment in which most routines and procedures do not change. They must know the structure of their routine so they can work for a given amount of time. That means reading at the same time every day, a chance to talk about their books, the knowledge of how to select their books, and how to get help if needed. I model and create scenarios for the reading workshop. I teach mini-lessons on what to do when you finish a book and how to write responses. I convey to students my expectations for when I am working with a few students and their role during this time. I also take time to monitor students while they are working. I may not be conferencing with a group but walking around telling participants what they are doing right and helping them to stay on task. This frees me up to work with students one-on-one or with small groups and allows other small groups to work with each other."

An important aspect of the workshop approach is the students' ability to read/write for a sustained period of time without becoming distracted or distracting others. Julie spends a great deal of time on mini-lessons about sustained reading. This includes how to choose "just right" books and what to do if others are distracting those around them. Together, Julie and her students generate a chart on how to pick "just right" books and ways in which distractions pull students from reading (see Figure 6.1). The discussion helps students become aware of their responsibility to others in the classroom. The students continue to add to the chart as new issues emerge over the first several weeks of school. The mini-lesson format provides a context for students to discuss distractions or book selection during reading time and ways to resolve any connected problems. As a result, the students participate in sustained reading for the remainder of the year.

SETTING UP THE CLASSROOM

As stated in Chapter 3, the physical arrangement of the classroom reflects a teacher's beliefs about literacy learning and should facilitate opportunities for students to engage in meaningful literacy activities. However, the size, shape, and furnishings of classrooms dictate, to a large degree, how they can be arranged. Julie's school is only 6 years old so her classroom is larger than some in older buildings. Yet, she still has some constraints. Her room is rectangular-shaped; one of the long walls has built-in coat closets, and the other has several large windows. She has

---

What makes a "just right" book?

Something you are interested in
Favorite authors
Can read most of the words
Reminds you of something in your past
Pictures/illustrations are good
Funny

What pulls us away from our reading?

Someone tries to show you something or asks you a question
Someone asks you for help with a word
Someone is reading too loud or is making noises
People walking around
Picking books that are not just right

FIGURE 6.1. Chart produced during mini-lessons on book selection and distractions during reading.

individual student desks rather than tables. Nevertheless, she works with what she has to make the best learning environment possible for her students.

When making decisions about classroom arrangements, keep in mind the following points:

➤ The reading center should be inviting, with a variety of genres arranged in a way that is easy to access and browse.

➤ There should be an area in which students can gather for whole-class instruction.

➤ There should be an area for small-group instruction in which guided reading books and assessment information are easily accessible.

➤ Desks should be arranged to facilitate collaborative learning.

➤ Resources such as paper, glue, pencils, sharpeners, dictionaries, and tape should be easily accessible to students.

➤ Bulletin boards should be used primarily for displaying student work (see Figure 6.2).

Additionally, Julie has a filing system in which she keeps students' writing folders and to which students have easy access. Furthermore, she has a place for students to turn in finished work and a place for graded papers, copies of newspa-

FIGURE 6.2. Student-centered bulletin boards.

pers, parent folders, and a volunteer basket. Keeping things labeled helps students, volunteers, and substitutes find what they need easily.

CREATING THE DAILY SCHEDULE

Just as the physical arrangement of a classroom is dictated by certain fixed attributes, so is the daily schedule. For Julie, the scheduling of "specials" (i.e., physical education, art, media center, computers, music), lunch, and recess are dictated by the school. Therefore, daily instructional time must work around them. Additionally, the amount of time spent teaching language arts and math is dictated by the district. Julie works with the other fourth-grade teachers to create the daily schedule (see Figure 6.3) beyond the required time slots:

"After penciling in the predetermined parts of the schedule, we pencil in the remaining subjects according to our prior knowledge of what has worked. For instance, we like the language arts block to be uninterrupted instead of 2 separate hours. We then have to work in math, since these are the two largest blocks. Next, we fit in science and social studies and start moving times to make that work. The next critical part is scheduling speech, occupational therapy, and the reading specialist—all students receiving these services must fit into the respective teachers' schedules and yet not be pulled out of important instructional times. We must also work with the special education collaboration teachers who are working with more than one classroom. You find yourself thinking that there just isn't enough time for everything."

Daily Schedule

9:10	Arrival, morning work
9:30	Specials (P.E., media center, art, music, computers)
10:15	Language arts
12:15	Recess
12:40	Lunch
1:20	Math
2:20	Social studies
2:55	Science
3:30	Dismissal

FIGURE 6.3. Sample fourth-grade daily schedule.

Creating a schedule that meets district, school, and student needs is an important part of effective instruction and involves more than just the individual classroom teacher (see the next section for more on creating a daily schedule).

COLLABORATIVE PLANNING FOR CURRICULAR INSTRUCTION

Julie has a very strong team of fourth-grade teachers that have been teaching together for the last 6 years. The teachers meet during specials on Wednesdays to plan the curriculum. Much of the content, scope, and sequence of what they teach is outlined in state and national standards. The district has created curriculum maps for each subject, which take the required standards for each grade level and arrange them into a suggested timeline. These maps include a list of skills that should be taught prior to benchmark testing for each 9-week grading period. The curriculum maps serve to organize what is taught and when. When Julie and the other fourth-grade teachers meet, they use the curriculum map as a guide but discuss ways to meet the needs of students and to integrate certain units of science and social studies with reading and writing.

On Fridays, the team meets to go over general housekeeping items, such as planning upcoming events, adjusting schedules for the following week for special programs or field trips, or to organize parent volunteers on certain projects. On the other days, team members informally meet to plan or share files about other subjects such as math. Julie's team "departmentalizes" social studies and science; that is, two teachers teach social studies to all fourth-grade students, and the other two teachers teach science. Therefore, this time is sometimes used by those who teach common subjects to plan, return phone calls, write notes to parents, or gather materials for the day. Julie reflects:

"Rarely do I get to grade papers or write lesson plans during my specials time. Besides these meetings, I have informal meetings with the special education teacher, who collaborates with me. This too is informal because this is what works for us. She attends the curriculum meetings with us but not the team meetings, because the special educations team meets at this time. Sometimes we troubleshoot activities ahead of time, and sometimes we brainstorm ideas for future units. We also talk about individual students and problems we need to work on."

Julie emphasizes the importance of grade-level teachers working together as a team to brainstorm solutions, share, and work with each other. Julie states:

"So much is required of teachers now that a strong supportive team is a must. This team shouldn't take away the teacher's individuality but help enhance his or her abilities to plan successfully and create the most for the students. I am very thankful to have the team with which I work."

WHAT DOES A DAY IN FOURTH GRADE LOOK LIKE?

The following section discusses each item on Julie's daily schedule.

Arrival

When children arrive in the morning, Julie has announcements, homework assignments and morning work written on the board. Julie explains:

"To start our day, when the children enter, they have homework assignments on the board to copy in their planner [discussed in the next chapter]. I then have morning work on the board that is to be completed or at least started. This helps to foster independence, gives me time to check with certain students, read notes, and talk to parents who happen to drop by with questions. The morning work is something that can be done independently. I like to vary it so it does not become routine. Sometimes it is journal writing, spelling patterns, or language skills. Sometimes it is a social studies newspaper to read or a math review. Sometimes students work on an assignment from the day before, such as a summary or reading journal reflection that they need to complete. Students always have the option of reading silently when they finish. I take the time to review any schedule changes or special activities for the day. I like to write these on the board so that students get used to reading directions and as a reminder of how their day may be different."

The morning routine sets the tone for the rest of the day. Students are learning to work independently and are engaged in meaningful learning from the very beginning of the school day.

Reading Workshop

The language arts block starts with the reading workshop, which consists of a mini-lesson, small-group lessons, one-on-one conferences, and independent reading. Each of these components was described at length in Chapter 3, so these descriptions will be brief. Julie's school does not use a basal program, so the texts used for instruction and independent/small-group reading are all authentic children's literature.

Mini-Lessons

Julie starts the reading workshop with a short whole-class mini-lesson. At the beginning of the year, the mini-lessons focus on management issues, such as how to interact with each other (creating community), how to select and care for books, how to choose "just right" books, how to keep a reading list, and how to write journal responses. As the year progresses and management of the reading workshop is underway, Julie focuses on reading strategies based on students' needs. An example of one of Julie's planning sheets for a reading workshop mini-lesson is presented in Figure 6.4.

Independent Reading and One-on-One Conferences

After the mini-lesson, students go to different areas of the room for independent reading. They are allowed to choose any spot in the room where they are comfortable. As students read independently, Julie conferences with individual students to learn about their interests, discuss their book choices, or check comprehension of the text they are reading. Julie will meet with all students in the course of a week and with students who need extra assistance more often.

At the end of the reading workshop, Julie gives students with whom she did not conference time to touch base with her. Julie reflects:

"They may come up and say, 'I really want to conference with you!', 'You were right, this book did get better in a few chapters,' 'Has this author written more books like this?', or 'My prediction was exactly right.' This little informal time gives them the opportunity to let me know what they are excited about if I didn't get to meet with them. Sometimes I'll tell them to make sure to let me know when they find out if something happens in the story that they predicted."

Focus: Setting

Read-aloud ideas:

Nonfiction: *What Is a Park?* [Trumbauer, 1999]

Poetry: "Grandmother's Brook"

Fiction:
- *Dinorella* [Edwards, 1997]
- *Prince Cinders* [Cole, 1987]
- *Cindy Ellen: A Wild Western Cinderella* [Lowell, 2000]
- *Stranger in the Woods* [Sams & Stoick, 2000]
- *Summertime in the Big Woods* [Wilder, 1996]

Mini-lesson focus: Understanding the importance of setting
- The setting is the time and place in which the story occurs.
- Good readers need to be aware of the use of "time" in their reading.
- Some authors move forward and backward through time, and that can be confusing to readers.
- Many writers use the techniques of "flashback" and "foreshadowing." In a flashback, readers journey back in time to read about things that happened earlier. Foreshadowing gives the readers a preview of what is to come. Many authors end a chapter by foreshadowing what is to happen next.
- We learn about setting through words and pictures.
- Setting is more important in some stories than others. Example: In *Hatchet* [Paulsen, 1987], the wilderness setting is integral to the story. However, sometimes setting is simply a backdrop for a story.
- Setting often influences the events in a person's life. Example: The rural setting influences Laura Ingalls Wilder [1935] in her *Little House* books.

FIGURE 6.4. Reading workshop mini-lesson planning sheet.

Individual conferencing is an important part of the reading workshop. The information Julie gains from each student informs her instruction of individuals as well as small-group and whole-class mini-lessons.

Small-Group Instruction

After Julie has had the opportunity to meet with students individually and assess their reading strengths and weaknesses, she forms flexible small groups. Julie gains knowledge of students' interests, comprehension strategies, and fluency from the groups formed at the beginning of the year. As the year progresses, initial groups disperse and new groups are formed based on student needs and interests (see Figure 6.5). Often, the groups are involved in response activities such as Readers' Theatre or performance poetry.

Writing Workshop

The writing workshop follows the same format as the reading workshop: whole-class mini-lesson, independent writing, individual conferencing, and small-group

FIGURE 6.5. A guided reading group engaged in a lively literature discussion.

instruction. At the beginning of the year, Julie has the students write personal narratives. Since the fourth-grade class consists of students who were in different third-grade classes, the students do not all know each other. Julie has students interview new classmates in pairs to gather information for the narrative. Mini-lessons are devoted to descriptions of how to develop the narrative. Inclusion students may have the special education teacher or assistant help as a third person in their group to take notes and interview.

As the year progresses, students are engaged in writing in a variety of genres and formats, often across the curriculum. Students write journal reflections in math, social studies, and science as well as seasonal writing for Halloween, Thanksgiving, and Christmas. In the spring, students write poetry, though they have been reading poetry throughout the year.

Word Study

Word study is conducted in small groups (see Figure 6.6) during a reading workshop or as a whole class at the beginning of language arts 1 or 2 days a week. Julie focuses on teaching students spelling patterns based on their developmental needs from her assessment of students' writing.

FIGURE 6.6. Small-group word study.

Read-Aloud

Each day Julie reads aloud to the children from a chapter book. It is her favorite time of the day, but more importantly, it is the children's favorite time of the day!

> "I try to read different genres; I start with realistic fiction, then historical fiction, and fantasy, and a mystery if there is time. I check student book orders and the public library for new ideas for read-alouds. Sometimes my students share a great title with me, or a guest speaker will give me a great book to read about his or her topic. I'm always on the lookout for a new book."

Julie's favorite read-alouds include *Shiloh* (1991, realistic fiction) by Phyllis Reynolds Naylor, *The Island of the Aunts* (2000, fantasy) by Eva Ibotson, and *A Lion to Guard Us* (1981, historical fiction) by Clyde Robert Bulla.

Math

The previous year, Julie's school district adopted a new math book, *Math Expressions*, published by Houghton Mifflin. One component of the new series is that students keep a math journal in which they write an explanation about how to work a problem or explain an answer to a word problem. The series has suggestions for journaling throughout the text. Journaling assists students with explaining verbally the process of how to solve a math problem instead of just getting the right answer. Julie also reads books that connect to different topics of the math curriculum. For example, she read *How Much Is a Million?* by David Schwartz (1985) when discussing place value and number sense.

Social Studies and Science

Julie is one of two teachers on her team who teaches social studies to all fourth-grade students. Therefore, she does not teach science. However, units are taught in science that tie into social studies, and vice versa, so often there is integration of the social studies and science, and all subjects are integrated with language arts. For example, Julie states:

> "Our weather unit has a read-aloud titled *Night of the Twisters* [Ruckman, 1984]. We have short nonfiction passages about weather events. Students study weather in science but also keep a journal about different weather patterns they observe during the unit. This happens for social studies, too. This is a great way to build vocabulary and illustrate words for word study. We teach reading skills such as identifying cause–effect relationships from nonfiction articles. Nonfiction is a big part of our strategy instruction across the curriculum in fourth grade."

When planning a social studies unit, Julie keeps in mind the concepts to be taught and how she can make them interesting to students (see Figure 6.7). She looks for books that are relevant and plans how to integrate them with reading and writing during the day. Julie does not use the social studies textbook to introduce a new unit. The difficulty of the text inhibits learning for most students. She prefers class time to be interactive and engaging. For example, she began a unit on Jamestown by asking students the following questions: "What type of people would you want to bring to start a colony in the new World? Why would you need these people?" This type of questioning involves students in critical thinking and engages them in the topic from the very start. Julie uses timelines and teaches vocabulary in context. She also engages students in many hands-on activities. She illustrates:

> "We list what kinds of things a soldier would take to war during the Civil War, and then I have a trunk of personal effects they might have taken (students don't think about toothbrushes, a Bible, or a journal). We have performed Patrick Henry's speech and debated what role we might have taken in the Revolutionary War: a soldier, a writer (like Thomas Jefferson), or a speaker (like Patrick Henry). Along with these activities, we watch videos and read picture-books."

VA Standards of Learning Objectives
- Understand that conflicts developed between the colonies and England over how the colonies should be governed.
- Understand that the Declaration of Independence gave reasons for independence and ideas for self-government.
- Identify reasons why colonists and the English Parliament disagreed over how the colonies should be governed.
- Understand that Virginians made significant contributions during the Revolutionary War.
- Identify varied roles of Virginians in the Revolutionary War era.

Daily Plan
Day 1: Understand the taxes imposed by England on the colonists.
Activities: Students play a simulation game using M&M's to represent taxes paid; students write a letter to King George to protest taxes.

Day 2: Understand how the colonies considered themselves separate and did not work together.
Activitiy: Groups research and make a flag from one of the 13 colonies.

Day 3: Groups finish making flags and share with the class. Read aloud *King George's Head Was Made of Lead* [Monjo, 1974], a true story about a revolt against the king.

Day 4: Understand the taxes the king imposed.
Activity: Students conduct research about the taxes on the Internet.

Day 5: Understand how the colonists prepared for war. Read aloud Patrick Henry's speech.
Activity: Students sign enlistment papers to join the Continental Army.

Day 6: Understand the strengths and weakness on both sides of the battle.

Day 7: Understand the context surrounding the creation and signing of the Declaration of Independence.
Activity: Students perform Readers' Theatre of Patrick Henry's speech.

Day 8: Explore the first battles of the Revolutionary War.

Day 9: Learn about George Washington.
Activities: Students read excerpts from *Winter at Valley Forge* [Knight, 1982]; watch video on George Washington.

Day 10: Students learn about famous Virginian patriots such as Jack Jouett and Thomas Jefferson.
Activity: Students write a paragraph about whether they would have used words as a weapon if they lived in this time period.

Day 11: Discuss the Battle of Yorktown and Colonel Cornwallis's surrender.

Day 12: Understand the effects the war had on the soldiers.
Activity: Use books from the library to scan for pictures of soldiers before and after Valley Forge and the Battle of Yorktown.

Included in This Unit
- Field trip to Yorktown
- Read-aloud novel: *Toliver's Secret* [Brady, 1976]
- Shared writing of daily journal of Revolutionary War figure during writing workshop
- Text sets of novels on the Revolutionary War read during reading workshop
- Poetry on the Revolutionary War introduced during reading workshop

FIGURE 6.7. Three-week unit plan for the Revolutionary War.

It's not until the end of the unit that Julie has the students read the textbook on the particular unit of study. Julie explains:

> "I have students read the chapter when their vocabulary and background knowledge are online. We also do picture walks with the book as part of the lesson. After students read the textbook, we share things as a group that they learned from the book. This is insightful for me because I can assess what they have learned. I do this in small groups and work with the captions and smaller articles instead of the whole text. I work with graphic organizers during this time, too."

An example of a graphic organizer, created by a small group of students on the causes of the Revolutionary War, appears in Figure 6.8. After Julie worked with the small group to create the graphic organizer, she worked with them on how to use

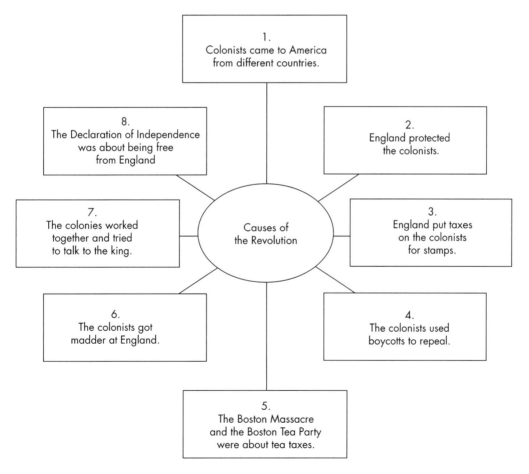

FIGURE 6.8. Students' information web on the causes of the Revolutionary War.

the graphic organizer to write a paper on the topic (see Figure 6.9). She showed the students how each numbered box in the organizer was a separate cause or topic of the war. She modeled how the students could turn the topic into a paragraph in their paper. The students worked together using the graphic organizer, the textbook, and various other texts and Internet sources to write a paper.

For inclusion students or students who struggle with reading and writing, Julie makes many other adjustments to her teaching to meet their needs:

> The social studies textbook comes with audiotapes of the chapters so that students can listen to the text read aloud.

> The inclusion collaboration teacher works with Julie to meet the needs of students with Individualized Education Plans (IEPs).

> For activities that involve more research and writing, such as writing a daily journal from the point of view of a character in the Revolutionary War, Julie

---

CAUSES OF THE REVOLUTION

People from all over Europe came to the new world to form the 13 colonies. Those 13 colonies later grew to all have the same problem . . . King George III!!

The French and Indian War led to the dession [sic] that the 13 colonies didn't need England anymore. After the colonies desided [sic] the king got furious.

George III was so high with rage that he passed a new act. This act is known as the Stamp Act. Colonists covered tax collectors in hot tar and feathers to show their rage.

The colonists boycotted the Townshend Act. Many things the colonists needed as in glass, paint, paper, lead and tea were taxed, too.

The patriots got ready to fight after a small argument occurred. Many people died in this fight! This was called the Boston Massacre.

The Sons of Liberty got mad at the taxes the king made them pay. The colonists got so mad at tea tax, they dumped hundreds of chests of tea into the Boston harbor.

Later the king passed many new taxes and the colonists ragaed [sic] with anger. Colonists wrote a letter to the king sying [sic] they want freedom. When the letter arrived, he ignored it!! When the colonists hear about that they wanted WAR!!!!

When they decided to have war not many people wanted to fight. About a year later a man named Patrick Henry gave a famous speech that the last words were . . . As for me, give me liberty or give me death!!

FIGURE 6.9. Research paper on causes of the Revolutionary War.

shortens the number of journal entries or provides alternative activities from which students can choose.

> For tests, Julie provides a concise study guide, a word bank, and reads the test aloud.

REVISITING WHAT WE KNOW ABOUT EFFECTIVE FOURTH-GRADE TEACHERS

The description of a day in Julie's fourth-grade classroom attempts to put into context the characteristics of effective instructional practices listed in Chapter 2 that develop high levels of reading proficiency while meeting students' needs. In the course of the day, Julie

> Taught students effective strategies for reading/writing nonfiction and content-area textbooks such as graphic organizers and vocabulary instruction.

> Provided differentiated instruction during reading/writing workshop, word study, and content area instruction in order to move each student's literacy forward.

> Used district curriculum maps as a guide for integrated instruction.

> Provided time for students to read and write independently every day. Students had the opportunity to self-select books of interest to them during the reading workshop from the classroom library.

> Provided explicit instruction during mini-lessons and content-area instruction, slowly releasing the responsibility for using the strategies to students during small-group and independent reading and writing.

> Provided students with multiple opportunities to learn new vocabulary through wide reading and direct instruction during the reading workshop and content-area instruction.

> Engaged students in literacy projects that integrated portions of the curriculum, such as journaling about different weather patterns over the course of the weather unit and reenacting Patrick Henry's speech.

> Provided students with multiple opportunities to engage in conversations with each other and with her across the curriculum.

> Did not use a scripted program, standardized lessons, or test preparation materials, but met students' needs through effective instruction.

Many aspects of teaching cannot be captured in a book. Nevertheless, this chapter attempted to convey more fully the multifaceted, complex nature of exemplary fourth-grade teaching. It is obvious from reading this chapter that to be an exemplary fourth-grade teacher requires professional responsibility, knowledge, commitment, and dedication.

CHILDREN'S LITERATURE

Brady E. (1976). *Toliver's secret*. New York: Crown.
Bulla, C. R. (1981). *A lion to guard us*. New York: Crowell.
Cole, B. (1987). *Prince Cinders*. New York: Putnam.
Edwards, P. (1997). *Dinorella*. New York: Hyperion.
Ibotson, E. (2000). *The island of the aunts*. New York: Dutton.
Knight, J. (1982). *Winter at Valley Forge*. Mahwah, NJ: Troll Associates.
Lowell, S. (2000). *Cindy Ellen: A wild western Cinderella*. New York: HarperCollins.
Monjo, F. (1974). *King George's head was made of lead*. New York: Putnam.
Naylor, P. R. (1991). *Shiloh*. New York: Atheneum.
Paulsen, G. (1987). *Hatchet*. New York: Simon & Schuster.
Ruckman, I. (1984). *Night of the twisters*. New York: Crowell.
Sams, C., & Stoick, J. (2000). *Stranger in the woods*. Miford, MI: Sams II Photography.
Schwartz, D. (1985). *How much is a million?* New York: Lothrop, Lee & Shepard.
Trumbauer, L. (1999). *What is a park?* New York: Rand McNally.
Wilder, C. (1996). *Summertime in the big woods*. New York: HarperCollins.
Wilder, L. I. (1935). *Little house on the prairie*. New York: Harper & Brothers.

CHAPTER 7

DEVELOPING HOME–SCHOOL PARTNERSHIPS THAT HELP CHILDREN LEARN

"What did you do?" I yelled. "What did you do to our poster?" It was covered all over with scribbles in every color of Magic Marker. It was ruined! . . . I grabbed my poster and ran into the kitchen to show it to my mother. I could hardly speak. "Look," I said, feeling a lump in my throat. "Just look at what he did to my poster." I felt tears come to my eyes but I didn't care. "How could you let him?" I asked my mother. "How? Don't you care about me?" (Blume, 1972, p. 38)

Yes, Fudge strikes again! He ruined Peter's homework project, which he and his two friends worked to complete for weeks, and Peter took out his frustration on his mother. Mrs. Hatcher bought Peter a new poster, and he and his friends reconstructed the piece better than the first time. After presenting the poster to the class, Mrs. Haver, their teacher, told them that they had done a super job.

As with Peter's family, parents of tweens not only have to deal with the changes in their relationships with their children, but they also have to confront a demanding fourth-grade curriculum, homework, and testing. Some parents need extensive guidance on how to work with their children; other parents, who were very involved in their child's classrooms in the primary grades, may not feel welcome now and need teachers to make an extended effort to invite them to participate. In all cases, it is critical that parents get involved in their child's education.

THE IMPORTANCE OF PARENTAL INVOLVEMENT IN FOURTH GRADE

Parental involvement is extremely important for children's literacy development. Results of the 2000 NAEP national reading assessment of fourth-grade students found the following correlations between reading scores and parental involvement:

> ➤ Students who reported more types of reading material at home scored higher than average; 68% of students who had three or more different types of reading materials at home performed at the proficient level, whereas students who had two or fewer types of reading material at home performed at the basic level. Students who had four types of reading materials at home performed the highest.

> ➤ Students who discussed their studies at home, however frequently, had higher average reading scores than students who reported never discussing their studies at home; 83% of students who discussed their studies once a month or more at home performed at the proficient level, compared to students who never, or hardly ever, discussed their studies at home and performed at the basic level.

> ➤ Students who talked about reading with family and friends, however frequently, had higher average scores than students who never, or hardly ever, talked about reading. Students who talked about reading once or twice a week performed the highest. (National Institute for Literacy, online document)

The NAEP results cross socioeconomic status, race, and gender. However, there is evidence that parental involvement is especially important for struggling readers and students at risk of failure. Cunningham and Allington (2007) report:

> Schools that have unusually high success rates with struggling readers are usually schools with high levels of family and community involvement. These schools make superhuman efforts to reach out to the parents and surrogate parents—aunts, cousins, grandmothers—and involve them in the school. Getting the parents of at-risk children to come to school is often not an easy task. Many of the parents did not succeed in school themselves, and their memories of school are not pleasant. Many of the parents have very limited literacy levels and many are not proficient in English. (p. 290)

All parents want their children to be successful in school. Exemplary fourth-grade teachers recognize parents and other adult caregivers as their strongest allies in the education of children.

BUILDING EFFECTIVE PARENT–TEACHER PARTNERSHIPS

It is very important for fourth-grade teachers to develop positive and mutually supportive relationships early in the school year with family members to achieve common goals for the literacy education of students. The next section offers suggestions for teachers to find out more about their students' literacy lives outside of school and to open communication and collaboration with students' families.

Bringing the Outside In: Family Literacy Projects

Effective teachers know that for students to be successful in the classroom, they must understand their students' lives outside of school. Teachers must inquire about students' language history, background, culture, reading interests, learning goals, and home life. This information can be gathered in several ways; for example, by (1) engaging in conversations with students (discussed in Chapter 3), (2) engaging in conversations with parents during parent–teacher conferences (discussed later in this chapter), (3) forming partnerships with community members, and (4) creating family literacy projects (see Figure 7.1 for more suggestions).

- Invite a community member to speak with the faculty and staff about the newcomers.

- Seek out religious and professional resources in your area (e.g., Illinois has the Illinois Resource Center, which is funded specifically to help educators deal with linguistic and cultural diversity in the state).

- Use the Internet to establish personal connections with educators in countries or regions from which your new student population has come to help you understand differences more easily.

- Read novels, children's books, and informational books about other cultures; use videos and CD-ROMs to extend knowledge as well.

- Create a cross-cultural committee of parents and community members to meet regularly with the faculty and staff to explore ways to learn more about, and become more sensitive to, one another.

- Connect either directly or online with other projects that are exploring cultural sensitivity.

- Make some home visits so that you can talk to parents in their home environment; such a visit can be a very important statement of your respect for them and your interest in their lives.

FIGURE 7.1. Focusing on family and community values. From Ogle (2007). Copyright 2007. Reprinted by permission.

The Trees of the Dancing Goats by Patricia Polacco (1996)
Jingle Dancer by Cynthia L. Smith (2000)
The Relatives Came by Cynthia Rylant (1985)
Where I'm From by George Ella Lyons (1999)
Coming to America: A Muslim Family's Story by Bernard Wolf (2003)
Neighborhood Odes by Gary Soto (1992)
Angelina's Island by Jeanette Winter (2007)

FIGURE 7.2. Examples of picturebooks about family memories/traditions.

Family literacy projects in which teachers can engage students to learn more about their background, culture, and home life include the following:

> *Family timelines.* Read aloud books about memories involving family and invite students to discuss and share their own memories. Then have students ask family members about important or memorable family events. Next students create a graphic family timeline of memories that includes illustrations or photographs to share with the class.

> *Family traditions class book.* Read aloud books in which family traditions are discussed (see Figure 7.2). Explore the meaning of family traditions and share your own family traditions with students. Then have students write and illustrate descriptions of their own unique family traditions. Each student's written and illustrated page is put together to create a class book.

> *Family read-aloud or storytelling.* Invite students' family members to read a favorite story or tell a story from their childhood or about their culture.

Family literacy projects involve students in authentic reading and writing experiences with the teacher, each other, and their families. The knowledge the teacher gains about the background, culture, and home life of each student can assist him or her in personalizing instruction and creating communities of practice in which students respect the knowledge and contributions of each other.

Ways to Involve Parents as Partners and Keep Communication Open

If families are to work with schools as partners in the education of their children, schools must provide them with the opportunities and support they need to become involved. Too often schools expect families to do it all alone. Developing effective partnerships with families requires that all school staff (administrators, teachers, and support staff) create a school environment that welcomes parents and encourages them to raise questions and voice their concerns as well as to participate appropriately in decision making. (U.S. Department of Education, 1997)

The expression "It takes a village" is an appropriate maxim for the level of involvement needed to create a successful partnership between families and schools. Teachers cannot do it alone. All school staff must reach out to parents with invitations to participate in their children's learning. In addition, school staff must play a role in providing parents with the information and training they need to become involved.

What Can Schools Do?

A review of successful family involvement programs by the U.S. Department of Education (1997) found that the most successful programs looked beyond the traditional definitions of parental involvement, such as participation in the PTA or back-to-school night, to a broader conception of parents as full partners in the education of their children. The *Family Involvement in Children's Education: An Idea Book*, compiled by the U.S. Department of Education (1997), describes successful strategies used by 20 local Title I programs that have overcome barriers to parental involvement. This idea book suggests ways in which schools, families, and communities can work together to build strong partnerships. It is organized around strategies for overcoming common barriers to family involvement in schools. These strategies include:

> *There is no "one-size-fits-all" approach to partnerships.* Build on what works well. Begin the school–family partnership by identifying, with families, the strengths, interests, and needs of families, students, and school staff, and design strategies that respond to these identified strengths, interests, and needs.

> *Training and staff development is an essential investment.* Strengthen the school–family partnership by providing professional development and training for all school staff as well as parents and other family members. Both school staff and families need the knowledge and skills that enable them to work with one another and with the larger community to support children's learning.

> *Communication is the foundation of effective partnerships.* Plan strategies that accommodate the varied language and cultural needs as well as lifestyles and work schedules of school staff and families. Even the best planned school–family partnerships will fail if the participants cannot communicate effectively.

> *Flexibility and diversity are key.* Recognize that effective parental involvement takes many forms that may not necessarily require parents' presence at a workshop, meeting, or school. Parents helping children learn is the goal, and it can happen in schools, homes, or elsewhere in a community.

> *Projects need to take advantage of the training, assistance, and funding offered by sources external to schools.* These sources may include school districts, community organizations and public agencies, local colleges and uni-

versities, state education agencies, and education-sponsored Comprehensive Regional Assistance Centers. Although Title I program funds support the parental involvement activities of many programs featured here, several learning communities have increased the resources available for parental involvement activities by looking beyond school walls.

➤ *Change takes time.* Recognize that developing a successful school–family partnership requires continued effort over time, and that solving one problem often creates new challenges. Furthermore, a successful partnership requires the involvement of many stakeholders, not just a few.

➤ *Projects need to regularly assess the effects of using multiple indicators.* These may include indicators of family, school staff, and community participation in, and satisfaction with, school-related activities. They may also include measures of the quality of school–family interactions and of student educational progress. (U.S. Department of Education, 1997)

Many organizations sponsor parental involvement in schools and offer a plethora of research, resources, and ideas for promoting family involvement. The following are a few:

➤ *The National Coalition for Parent Involvement in Education* (NCPIE; *ncpie. org*). The mission of NCPIE is to serve as a visible representative for strong parent and family involvement initiatives at the national level. The organization conducts activities and provides resources and legislative information that can help promote parent and family involvement.

➤ *Parent Teacher Association* (PTA; *www.pta.org*). The majority of schools across the United States have a PTA. In 1997 the PTA set standards for parent and family involvement programs. The website houses many resources for parents and teachers.

➤ *Colorado Parent Information and Resource Center* (CPIRC; *www.cpirc.org*). The CPIRC is one of 28 parental assistance centers across the United States funded by the Department of Education. The comprehensive website houses information for parents and those who work with parents. The site includes over 100 tip sheets and reviews of state and national projects and research on parental involvement.

➤ *The Parent Involvement Institute* (PII; *www.par-inst.com/educator*). The mission of the PII is to encourage parental involvement in the education of children. The PII publishes a variety of materials, including newsletters, booklets, brochures, and videos.

➤ *Parental Information and Resource Centers* (PIRCs; *www.ed.gov/programs/ pirc/index.html*). Funded by the U.S. Department of Education, PIRCs help implement successful and effective parental involvement policies, programs, and activities that lead to improvements in students' academic achievement and that strengthen partnerships among parents, teachers, principals, administrators, and other school personnel in meeting the educational needs of children.

Additionally, schools can make sure parents are aware of resources available to them for participating in literacy activities with their children. The following are a few suggestions:

➢ *Book resources.* Schools can inform parents of resources available for accessing books for their children. Discount bookstores, yard sales, and public library book sales are inexpensive ways for parents to purchase books. Scholastic Book Clubs are popular with teachers, and parents may remember buying books through Scholastic orders when they were in school. Scholastic has a parental program that allows parents to purchase books directly. Scholastic carries a variety of books at different grade levels and at (usually) cheaper prices than bookstores (*www.clubs.scholastic.com*).

➢ *Book discussions.* Many public libraries and bookstores have weekly, biweekly, or monthly book club meetings in which parents and children can discuss books in a group setting.

➢ *Online book discussions.* Parents and children can also participate in online book discussions. Sometimes called *book raps* or *book chats*, book discussions are online discussion groups about books that take place using e-mail, chat rooms, or discussion boards. Classes from different parts of the world can read and discuss books together. At the same time students can learn about culture and diversity. The following are a few online sources:

  ➢ *Raps* (*www.learningplace.com.au/raps.asp?orgid=79&suborgid=497*). Contains a variety of raps (discussions of a book, movie, piece of music, or game) in which parents can register their children to participate. Most raps last 4–6 weeks.

  ➢ *The Spaghetti Book Club* (*www.spaghettibookclub.com*). Program in which students read and study books and write, edit, and publish book reviews. The website contains many book reviews written by students.

  ➢ *Book Raps* (*www.rite.ed.qut.edu.au/old_oz-teachernet/projects/book-rap/index1.html*). Gives information about book raps, including definition, expected outcomes, and resources.

  ➢ *Book BackChats* (*www.english.unitecnology.ac.nz/bookchat/home.php*). Website contains discussions on books. Facilitators ask questions that the participants answer. Around five new book discussions are started each term.

  ➢ *BookChat* (*www.cgps.vic.edu.au/bookchat/home.htm*). Website that allows students to sign up to chat about books. Also contains activities for students.

What Can Teachers Do?

Over the course of Julie's teaching career, she has worked tirelessly to collaborate with parents. Her experiences can provide invaluable insight to other fourth-grade teachers. Julie provides her top 10 suggestions for collaborating with parents and other caregivers:

1. Encourage contact by giving parents your home/school phone numbers and e-mail address and let them know you are available for them. Be relaxed and positive when talking with parents. They are nervous, too.

2. Follow up promptly to notes, messages, and requests/questions.

3. Let parents know how they can be involved in helping their child study for tests, ensuring that homework is completed, or letting you know when homework is too difficult.

4. Be very clear about directions for completing assignments/projects and due dates.

5. Listen to what parents have to share with you about their child.

6. Ask questions to help you understand their child better or to clarify your understanding of any situation.

7. Offer suggestions to help parents when they are having difficulty with their child.

8. Follow up after discussing a problem and solution.

9. Encourage parents to "hang in there" and keep trying.

10. *Thank* parents for all their hard work and let them know you appreciate them!

By keeping these suggestions in mind, teachers can open mutually supportive communication with parents, making them feel welcome and included. Ways in which teachers can provide ongoing two-way communication with parents throughout the school year include the following:

➢ *Initial and weekly phone calls.* Contact all parents at the beginning of the school year to extend a warm welcome and introduction. Then, every week, make positive phone calls to let parents know their child had a great day, reached a goal, passed a test, or made a wonderful presentation in class. Teachers can make several phone calls in 10–15 minutes and send an important message to parents about all the positive things their children are doing in school.

➢ *Parent questionnaire.* Send a questionnaire home to parents requesting information about ways in which they can contribute to the classroom (see a sample questionnaire in Figure 7.3). This is an easy and effective way to extend an invitation and involve parents in a variety of ways in the classroom.

Child's name: _____

Name of parent willing to help _____

Phone number _____ **Home language** _____

I would like to help with the activities in my child's classroom. (Please place a check on the lines next to what you are interested in helping with.)

____ **Reading**	____ **Writing**	____ **Math**	____ **Science**
____ Reading to children	____ Help publish	____ Work with small group	____ Help with experiments
____ Conference with kids	____ Edit	____ Other	____ Other
____ Other	____ Other		
____ History/social studies	____ **Art**	____ **Music**	____ **PE**
____ Work with projects	____ Teach a lesson	____ Teach a lesson	____ Teach a lesson
____ Other	____ Other	____ Other	____ Other

I would rather help the teacher in the class with

____ Making journals   ____ Making children's books   ____ Making copies
____ Cutting and pasting   ____ Decorating the room   ____ Anything

I would like to help with preparing these materials at home _____

I would like to help with special events:

____ Class parties and celebrations   ____ Field trips
____ Author's tea   ____ Other

I would like to be classroom mom _____ (coordinate events with all the parents and the teacher)

I have a special talent I would like to share with the class: _____
(e.g., Cook, build models, sew, paint, tell stories)

I am a _____ (e.g., nurse, author, gardener, veterinarian). **Please call on me when my expertise could be of help with any unit of study or if you need something that has to do with my profession.** _____

I can help: Before school _____ After school _____ Any time _____
During: Early morning: 8:00–10:00 A.M. _____ Only at this time: _____
             Late morning: 10:00–12:00 P.M. _____ Only at this time: _____
During the afternoon: 12:45–2:45 P.M. _____ Only at this time: _____

I can help on these days:
___Monday __ Tuesday ___Wednesday ___Thursday ____ Friday ___ Any day

Please call me as a substitute or on an as-needed basis _____

FIGURE 7.3. Survey of parents for helping in the classroom. From Cappellini (2005). Copyright 2005 by Stenhouse. Reprinted by permission.

➤ *Family message journals.* Students keep journals in which they write a message to their family, focusing on classroom learning and activities they have participated in during the day. Students take the journal home, read the message to their family, and write a reply. Family message journals serve as an authentic way for students to engage in writing, reflect on their own learning, and inform parents about their daily learning and activities.

➤ *E-mail list.* Almost everyone uses e-mail these days. By making a mailing list with parents' e-mails, teachers can help keep parents informed. Send a weekly e-mail containing school events, dates of quizzes and tests, activities going on in class, and resources such as books or Internet links about curriculum topics. Students whose parents do not have an e-mail address can take home a printout of the e-mail.

➤ *Friday folders.* Folders can be sent home at the end of each week containing important forms, notes, events, and graded assignments. By including a place for parents' signatures and written feedback, teachers can ensure that parents receive the folders and also receive questions or comments in return from parents. Friday folders (or any day of the week) are a great way to establish two-way communication with parents.

➤ *Newsletter.* Sending regular newsletters can be a great way to keep parents informed by outlining upcoming events, asking for parent volunteers, describing current units of study and/or specific supplies needed, listing teachers' contact information, and much more. A newsletter can increase parent and child communication at home and keep parents informed (see Figure 7.4 for a sample newsletter).

➤ *Homework assignment sheet.* Homework can be difficult for both parents and children. A homework assignment sheet, signed each day by the parent and the child, serves as a reminder and as an accountability measure. Julie's school provides all students with a planner. Her students write homework assignments in the planner each day, and parents sign the planner each night indicating that they have seen the homework assignment.

At the beginning of the school year, during open house, the fourth-grade teachers discuss their philosophy and guidelines for homework with parents via a PowerPoint presentation. In this way, the purpose of homework and expectations for teachers, parents, and students are clearly communicated. A printout of the presentation is given to all parents in attendance and sent home to all parents who were unable to attend (see Figure 7.5).

➤ *Web page.* Most schools have websites on which individual teachers have a classroom page. Teachers can have the same information as newsletters or other forms of communication, but with the advantage that parents, grandparents, relatives, and family friends around the world have access. Student projects, writing, or other products can be scanned and placed on the Web page to show family and friends anywhere.

Dear Parents,

It's hard to believe that the school year is winding down. We still have so much to do! Please remember that Monday, Memorial Day, there is no school. When we return on Tuesday, May 27, we will have our author's celebration in the morning. Each child will go to a staff person in our school. He or she will be mixed with other children from other grades and classes. Because we use all of our support staff, each group will only have eight children. During their celebration, we will share our writing and do a writing activity. I am looking forward to this fun morning. On Friday, May 30, we will have field day in the afternoon. Let's hope that we have a day of sunshine and good sportsmanship for all the classes.

We have had a good time studying World War II this week in social studies. It has been exciting watching the small groups working with researching topics in class for a Friday share session. We have been looking at Virginia's role during the war. Such topics such as rationing and women's roles have surprised the groups. I am impressed with the way the groups are working together and sharing information. On Friday, we will hopefully learn many facts about the war. We have also been creating war enlistment posters to share on that day. Our science unit on plants is continuing to move along.

We have been reading *Tall Tales* in our reading workshop and having fun with exaggeration. Once you get used to the crazy phrases, it is easy to use exaggeration for anything you want to say! Please remember to have your child read throughout the summer. Children are very good at picking out appropriate books of high interest. A short trip to the library on a regular basis will keep them supplied. The bookmobile also visits many neighborhoods. It is so important to read on a regular basis throughout these summer months. So please, set aside a little time each day for this worthwhile activity. What a great way to cool down or relax at the end of a busy day of playing. Enjoy your weekend!

Mrs. Lipscomb

FIGURE 7.4. Sample newsletter.

Homework without Tears

Why Homework?
- Provides students with opportunities to deepen their understanding and skills relative to content.
- Extends learning opportunities beyond the confines of the school day.
- Teaches students to develop self-discipline and good study habits.
- Gives parents the opportunity to get involved with their children's education.

Does Homework Help Children Learn?
Yes! Research in recent years has suggested that homework does positively influence the achievement of elementary students.

Types of Homework
- Practice (e.g., reading journal)
- Preparation (e.g., multiplication and division facts)
- Projects (e.g., science fair)

Fourth Grade's Homework Policy
- Homework is assigned Monday through Thursday.
- Students are expected to turn in all assignments on time.
- Students who fail to turn in assignments will go to study hall to complete assignments. Any work not completed in study hall will be sent home (students do not miss recess to complete homework).
- Homework consists of:
  - Reading: 20 minutes of reading nightly and writing in journal
  - Math: nightly practice of math facts
  - Writing: weekly writing assignment
  - Projects
  - Studying for tests
  - Occasionally, social studies and science homework

What is NOT an Acceptable Excuse for Not Completing Homework
- "I played a sport last night and I didn't have time."
- "I started too late and it was way past my bedtime."
- "I had somewhere to go."
- "My dog ate the paper."
- "I did it, but it is at home."

It's All about RESPONSIBILITY!
Homework success is only achieved when teachers, parents, and students work together. We all have a share in the responsibility when it comes to homework.

(continued)

FIGURE 7.5. Handout on homework given to parents at open house *(page 1 of 2)*.

From *Teaching Literacy in Fourth Grade* by Denise Johnson. Copyright 2008 by The Guilford Press. Permission to photocopy this figure is granted to purchasers of this book for personal use only (see copyright page for details).

Teacher's Responsibility

- Provide meaningful assignments designed to help develop students' knowledge and skills.
- Provide clear instructions as to how the homework assignment should be completed.
- Ensure that assignments are matched to students' ability.
- Provide constructive feedback on assignments.

Parent's Responsibility

- Act as homework facilitator.
- Check over completed assignments and sign off in the planner.
- Give praise and encouragement.
- Read once a week out loud with your child and sign the log.

Student's Responsibility

- Be able to explain assignment—what is expected and what should be completed.
- Neatly complete all assignments.
- Place assignments in binder/backpack.
- Turn in assignments on time.

How Can You Help?

- Encourage, motivate, and prompt your child to do quality work.
- Help set up a consistent, organized place for homework to be done.
- Establish a consistent schedule for completing homework assignments.
- Establish a schedule with your child to complete long-term assignments/projects.
- Notify your child's teacher of any difficulties in completing assignments.

When to Call It a Night

- If your child is completely frustrated with the assignment.
- It is taking your child much too long to complete the homework.

FIGURE 7.5. (page 2 of 2)

Ways to Encourage Parents to Become Involved in Their Child's Reading Life

Parent–Teacher Conferences

Parent–teacher conferences are usually held between two and four times a year in most elementary schools in the United States. Unfortunately, these conferences have typically constituted the primary form of communication between parents and teachers. However, they can serve as an important means of communication when careful consideration is given to the planning and structure of the conferences. Julie provides the following suggestions for scheduling, conducting, and following up on parent–teacher conferences.

➢ *Prior to scheduling conferences* send a note home asking parents to tell you what they want to find out at the conference—for example, trouble with homework, social issues, note taking, test taking, making friends. This way you will be prepared to address all concerns.

➢ *Schedule conferences and gather materials.* Schedule conferences with all students, not just those who may be having difficulty. It is just as important to conference with the parents of students who are doing really well because they need to know what their child's strong points are and where he or she shines. It helps to build rapport and establish communication.

Showing parents their child's strengths/weaknesses in particular areas during the conference via examples of the student's work is strongly recommended. Using rubrics for grading also can be helpful when discussing areas of strengths and weaknesses (see Figure 7.6 for an example of a reading workshop scoring rubric). Organize samples of students' work and test results so that they are easily accessible and will complement the conference plan. Write down the topics you will discuss.

➢ *Include students in the conference.* It can be very helpful to include the student in the conference. It lets the student know that his or her success is the parents' and teacher's main concern—they are on the same side and are talking to keep one another informed.

➢ *Avoid educational jargon.* Teachers have to remember not to talk over parents' heads or intimidate them in any way. I consider the teacher and parent as partners for the year. Parents possess insightful information about their children and their history in school, and we need them to reinforce what students are learning, help with homework, and value the importance of school and education. We need each other!

➢ *Start off on a positive note.* Start the conference with a compliment about the student. As a parent, I know parents feel very nervous about what the teacher is going to say. It helps to break the ice and lets them know that I value their child. I also begin with what the child is doing well and where his or her strengths lie.

Key elements	5 Points	4 Points	3 Points	2 Points
Mini-lesson	Consistently demonstrates understanding of concepts	Usually demonstrates understanding of concepts	Sometimes demonstrates understanding of concepts	Rarely demonstrates understanding of concepts
	Always participates in mini-lesson	Usually participates in mini-lesson	Sometimes participates in mini-lesson	Rarely participates in mini-lesson
Reading/ conferring	Consistently selects quality books at appropriate level	Usually selects books at appropriate level	Sometimes selects books at appropriate level	Has difficulty choosing books at appropriate level
	Consistently identifies the genre of the book he/she is reading	Usually identifies the genre of the book he/she is reading	Sometimes identifies the genre of the book he/she is reading	Never identifies the genre of the book he/she is reading
	Consistently reads independently and uses time wisely	Usually reads independently and uses time wisely	Sometimes reads independently and uses time wisely	Rarely reads independently
	Demonstrates clear understanding through discussion/retelling	Demonstrates general understanding; can retell most of the important points	Inconsistently demonstrates general understanding; can retell some of the important points	Demonstrates little understanding; prompting needed in retelling
	Consistently uses reading strategies	Usually uses reading strategies	Sometimes uses reading strategies	Rarely uses reading strategies
	Consistently completes books	Usually completes books	Sometimes completes books	Usually abandons books
Journaling	Consistently completes journal when assigned	Usually completes journal when assigned	Sometimes completes journal when assigned	Rarely completes journal when assigned
	Consistently writes quality entries	Usually writes quality entries	Sometimes writes quality entries	Rarely writes quality entries
Take-home reading	Consistently reads for the required amount of time and completes home reading log	Usually reads for the required amount of time and completes home reading log	Sometimes reads for the required amount of time and completes home reading log	Rarely reads for the required amount of time or completes home reading log
Total Points	_____ /55 Comments:			

FIGURE 7.6. Intermediate reading workshop rubric. From Orehovec and Alley (2003). Copyright 2003 by Scholastic. Reprinted by permission.

➤ *Take the opportunity to learn more about students.* Asking parents simple questions such as "Can you tell me about your child?" and "How do you think I can best help your child learn?" changes the purpose of the conference from a transmission of information from teacher to parents to one in which the teacher and parents are sharing information in an effort to move learning forward.

➤ *Offer strategies for solving issues.* I always offer strategies that may help with problem areas. Usually parental input is very helpful in deciding what kind of solution will work. For example, if the student doesn't understand directions clearly, I offer to write notes in the student's planner or at the top of the page. Then we work out an agreement to each sign off that we have seen the planner. Suggestions regarding preparing for tests include studying more than one night and making flash cards. Also, I can sometimes help parents understand the type of structure and environment needed for studying. I offer assistance where possible on the school front, and we agree to touch base in a few weeks to see if the strategies are working or if more are needed.

➤ *End the conference.* I always try to end the conference on a very positive note. I recap what decisions we have made and let parents know that I will touch base at a later time to see how things are working at home. Parents are usually very willing to try to work out solutions that might help their children, especially if they sense the teacher really cares. Sometimes parents blame themselves for their child's difficulty in school (e.g., "I've been really busy at work"), but I try to move past the blame by commenting that everyone has circumstances that are not ideal and each family needs to learn to work with its situation.

➤ *Follow up in some manner.* Thank the family via a phone call, written note, or e-mail for attending the conference, inquire about follow-through with recommended strategies, and extend an open invitation to call with any questions that may have arisen after the conference.

MAKING THE CONNECTION

As discussed throughout the chapters in the book, students in fourth grade are experiencing a time of transition in their physical, emotional, social, and academic lives. Parental involvement is key to understanding and supporting students throughout the school year. The suggestions in this chapter offer numerous ways to create two-way communication that will influence classroom instruction and the support students receive at home. Positive, mutually supportive collaboration with parents is the best way to ensure the achievement of common goals for the literacy development of all students.

REFERENCES

Cappellini, M. (2005). *Balancing reading and language learning.* Portland, ME: Stenhouse.

Cunningham, P., & Allington, R. (2007). *Classrooms that work: They can all read and write.* New York: Allyn & Bacon.

National Institute for Literacy. (2007). *Parental involvement in learning.* Washington, DC: Author. Retrieved July 12, 2007, from *www.nifl.gov/nifl/facts/parental.html*

Ogle, D. (2007). *Coming together as readers* (2nd ed.). Thousand Oaks, CA: Corwin Press.

Orehovec, B., & Alley, M. (2003). *Revisiting the reading workshop: Management, mini-lessons, and strategies.* New York: Scholastic.

U.S. Department of Education. (1997). *Family involvement in children's education: An idea book.* Washington, DC: Author. Retrieved October 7, 2007, from *www.ed.gov/pubs/FamInvolve/execsumm.html*

CHILDREN'S LITERATURE

Blume, J. (1973). *Tales of a fourth-grade nothing.* New York: Dutton.

Lyons, G. E. (1999). *Where I'm from.* Springs, TX: Absey & Co.

Polacco, P. (1996). *The trees of the dancing goats.* New York: Simon & Schuster.

Rylant, C. (1985). *The relatives came.* New York: Bradbury Press.

Smith, C. L. (2000). *Jingle dancer.* New York: Morrow.

Soto, G. (1992). *Neighborhood odes.* San Diego, CA: Harcourt Brace Jovanovich.

Winter, J. (2007). *Angelina's island.* New York: Farrar, Straus & Giroux.

Wolf, B. (2003). *Coming to America: A Muslim family's story.* New York: Lee & Low.

CHAPTER 8

RESOURCES AND MORE

Exemplary fourth-grade teachers have been characterized throughout the chapters in this book as influential motivators and coaches who use their knowledge of child development, assessment information, and effective teaching strategies to move children's literacy learning forward. Exemplary teachers also continue to develop professional expertise. This chapter presents print and Internet resources that will assist you in expanding your professional knowledge about classroom instructional materials and sources for professional development. These resources are offered as a sample of available sources of information and materials, not as an exhaustive list.

CLASSROOM RESOURCES FOR TEACHERS AND STUDENTS

Throughout this book I have emphasized the use of children's literature—books that children can read and are interested in reading—to motivate students to read. The resources in this section provide teachers with information on children's literature, lists of fiction and nonfiction books appropriate for fourth graders, and supplemental materials for content-area reading. In addition to your school librarian and local public librarian, these resources can help you select quality literature and content-area materials for instruction and for your classroom library.

General Resources on Children's Literature

Lattimer, H. (2003). *Thinking through genre: Units of study in reading and writing workshops 4–12.* Portland, ME: Stenhouse.

Opitz, M., Ford, M., & Zbaracki, M. (2006). *Books and beyond: New ways to reach readers.* Portsmouth, NH: Heinemann.

Reutzel, R., & Fawson, P. (2002). *Your classroom library: New ways to give it more teaching power.* New York: Scholastic.

Roser, N., & Martinez, M. (Eds.). *What a character! Character study as a guide to literacy meaning making in grades K–8.* Newark, DE: International Reading Association.

Silvey, A. (2004). *100 Best books for children.* New York: Houghton Mifflin.

Children's Literature Web Guide (*www.ucalgary.ca/~dkbrown/awards.html*).—Provides a comprehensive guide to award-winning English-language children's books as well as Internet resources related to books for children and young adults.

Database of Award-Winning Children's Literature (DAWCL; *www.dawcl.com/introduction.html*).—One way to find quality multicultural children's literature is by locating books that have won awards. Yet, knowing about and finding all of the awards can be an arduous task. Not anymore! DAWCL has a database of almost 6,000 books connected to 73 awards across six English-speaking countries. The database allows the user to create a tailored reading list of quality children's literature or to find out if a book has won one of the indexed awards.

International Reading Association's Teacher's, Children's, and Young Adult's Choices Lists (*www.reading.org/resources/tools/choices.html*).—Free download of each of the lists.

Engaging with Literature 3–5 (*www.learner.org/resources/series182.html?pop=yes& vodid=397319&pid=1980#*).—This video library includes nine 20-minute videos that give language arts teachers and other educators an opportunity to observe firsthand how their peers are successfully guiding students in grades 3–5 toward becoming more active and involved readers of literature.

Picturebooks

Picturing Books (*www.picturingbooks.imaginarylands.org*).—An amazing website that provides information and resources on every aspect of the picturebook.

100 Picturebooks Everyone Should Know (*www.kids.nypl.org/reading/recommended2. cfm?ListID=61*).—An annotated list sponsored by the New York Public Library.

Themed Reviews of Wordless Picturebooks (*www.childrenslit.com/th_wordless.html*).—An annotated list of 50 wordless picturebooks sponsored by the Children's Literature website.

Caldecott Medal (*www.ala.org*).—The American Library Association (ALA) annually bestows the prestigious Caldecott Medal to the picturebook with the most outstanding illustrations. Information on past winners and honor books, plus other resources, are available on the ALA site.

Charlotte Zolotow Award (*www.education.wisc.edu/ccbc/authors/lecture/czlecture. asp*).—In 1998 the Cooperative Children's Book Center (CCBC) established the

Charlotte Zolotow Lecture and Award for outstanding writing in a picturebook. The CCBC site houses webcasts of the winners' lectures, including those of Angela Johnson, Linda Sue Park, Kevin Henkes, and Katherine Paterson.

Fantasy and Science Fiction

Levine, G. (2006). *Writing magic: Creating stories that fly.* New York: HarperCollins.

Marcus, L. (2006). *The wand in the word: Conversations with writers of fantasy.* Cambridge, MA: Candlewick Press.

The Science Fiction and Fantasy Bibliography (www.sfbooklist.co.uk).—A database of over 200 science fiction and fantasy authors with links to websites and book information.

The Golden Duck Awards for Excellence in Science Fiction (www.goldenduck.org).— These awards are given in the categories of picturebooks, middle grades, and young adults. This site lists the criteria for the award along with online resources for teachers to promote the use of science fiction in the classroom.

Historical Fiction

Tunnell, M., & Ammon, R. (1993). *The story of ourselves: Teaching history through children's literature.* Portsmouth, NH: Heinemann.

Scott O'Dell Award for Historical Fiction (www.scottodell.com/sosoaward.html).—In 1982 Scott O'Dell established the Scott O'Dell Award for Historical Fiction. The annual award of $5,000 goes to a meritorious book published in the previous year for children or young adults. Scott O'Dell established this award to encourage other writers—particularly new authors—to focus on historical fiction. He hoped in this way to increase the interest of young readers in the historical background that has helped to shape their country and their world.

Historical Fiction Book Lists (www.bookgirl3.tripod.com/historicalfiction.html).—If you are looking for a historical fiction book, this is the site to visit. Books are categorized by continent and subdivided by countries or historical eras. Each country/ era book list is divided by grade level. A cover picture of the book, a synopsis, and number of pages are provided for each entry.

Poetry

Heard, G. (1999). *Awakening the heart: Exploring poetry in elementary and middle school.* Portsmouth, NH: Heinemann.

Holbrook, S. (2005). *Practical poetry: A nonstandard approach to meeting content-area standards.* Portsmouth, NH: Heinemann.

National Council of Teachers of English Resource Page for Poetry (www.ncte.org/collections/poetry).—Includes teaching strategies for reading, writing, and performing poetry; links to articles and book chapters; and other online resources.

Lee Bennett Hopkins Promising Poet Award (*www.reading.org/association/awards/childrens_hopkins.html*).—This is a $500 award given every 3 years to a promising new poet who writes for children and young adults, and who has published no more than two books of children's poetry. A book-length single poem may be submitted. ("Children's poetry" is defined as poetry, rather than light verse.) The award is for published works only. Poetry in any language may be submitted; non-English poetry must be accompanied by an English translation.

NCTE Award for Poetry for Children (*www.ncte.org/about/awards/sect/elem/106857.htm*).—The National Council of Teachers of English wishes to recognize and foster excellence in children's poetry by encouraging its publication and by exploring ways to acquaint teachers and children with poetry through such means as publications, programs, and displays. As one means of accomplishing this goal, NCTE established its Award for Excellence in Poetry for Children in 1977 to honor a living American poet for his or her aggregate work for children ages 3–13. The NCTE Poetry Selection Committee gave the award annually until 1982, at which time it was decided that the award would be given every 3 years.

Nonfiction

Duke, N., & Bennett-Armistead, S. (2003). *Reading and writing informational text in the primary grades: Researched-based practices.* New York: Scholastic.

Hoyt, L., Mooney, M., & Parkes, B. (2003). *Exploring informational texts: From theory to practice.* Portsmouth, NH: Heinemann.

Moss, B. (2003). *Exploring the literature of fact: Children's nonfiction trade books in the elementary classroom.* New York: Guilford Press.

Stead, T. (2006). *Reality checks: Teaching reading comprehension with nonfiction K–5.* Portland, ME: Stenhouse.

Zarnowski, M. (2003). *History makers: A questioning approach to reading and writing biographies.* Portsmouth, NH: Heinemann.

Booklist's On-line Nonfiction Series Roundup (*www.ala.org/ala/booklist/youthseriesroundup/SeriesRoundup.htm*).—The online Series Roundup is the digital counterpart to *Booklist's* print coverage of the nonfiction series. Reviews consist of series titles that were recommended in the print magazine, starting with the April 15, 2004, issue, as well as selected reviews from previous years, and the list will be continually updated with reviews of series nonfiction that appear in the magazine throughout the year. All series books have been evaluated and recommended by children's book specialists.

Orbis Pictus Nonfiction Award (*www.ncte.org/about/awards/sect/elem/106877.htm*).—The Orbis Pictus award, given by the National Council of Teachers of English, is an annual award for promoting and recognizing excellence in the writing of nonfiction for children. The name *Orbis Pictus* commemorates the work of Johannes

Amos Comenius, *Orbis Pictus—The World in Pictures* (1657), considered to be the first book actually planned for children.

Robert F. Sibert Informational Book Medal (*www.ala.org*).—This award, established by the Association for Library Service to Children in 2001, is awarded annually to the author (including coauthors or author–illustrators) of the most distinguished informational book published in English during the preceding year.

Boston Globe Horn Book Awards for Nonfiction (*www.hbook.com/awards/bghb/default. asp*).—First presented in 1967 and customarily announced in June, the Boston Globe Horn Book Awards are among the most prestigious honors in the field of children's and young adult literature. Winners are selected in three categories: picturebook, fiction and poetry, and nonfiction. Two Honor Books may be named in each category. On occasion, a book will receive a special citation for its high quality and overall creative excellence. The winning titles must be published in the United States, but they may be written or illustrated by citizens of any country. The awards are chosen by an independent panel of three judges who are annually appointed by the editor of the Horn Book.

Children's Book Guild Award for Nonfiction (*www.childrensbookguild.org/awardnonfiction. htm*).—The *Washington Post* Children's Book Guild Award for Nonfiction honors an author or author–illustrator whose total work has contributed significantly to the quality of nonfiction for children. Nonfiction is written or illustrated work that arranges and interprets documented facts intended to illuminate, without imaginative invention, the following fields of knowledge: science, technology, social science, history, biography, and the arts.

Multicultural and International Children's Literature

Ada, A. (2003). *A magical encounter: Latino children's literature in the classroom* (2nd ed.). Boston: Allyn & Bacon

Hansen-Krening, N. (2003). *Kaleidoscope: A multicultural booklist for grades K–8* (4th ed.). Urbana, IL: National Council of Teachers of English.

Henderson, D., & May, J. (2005). *Exploring culturally diverse literature for children and adults: Learning to listen in new ways.* Boston: Pearson.

Seale, D., & Slapin, B. (Eds.). (2005). *A broken flute: The native experience in books for children.* Lanham, MD: AltaMira Press.

The USBBY-CBC International Children's Books Honor List (*www.usbby.org/biblioctte. html*).—In 2006 the United States Board on Books for Young People (USBBY) and the Children's Book Council (CBC) introduced a new bibliography of outstanding books originally published outside the United States. The 42 books chosen for the honor list range from K–12.

Multicultural Children's Literature (*www.multiculturalchildrenslit.com*).—This website contains links to annotated bibliographies of children's multicultural books appropriate for the elementary grades (K–6). Cultural groups currently listed include African Americans, Chinese Americans, Latino/Hispanic Americans, Japanese Americans, Jewish Americans, Native Americans, and Korean Americans.

Growing Up around the World: Books as Passports to Global Understanding for Children in the United States (*www.ala.org/ala/alsc/alscresources/booklists/GrowingUpAroundWorld. htm*).—As a project of the International Relations Committee of the Association for Library Service to Children, the purpose of this project is to make books that accurately depict contemporary life in other countries more widely available to American children. The project includes bibliographies representing five regions: Africa, the Americas, Asia and the Middle East, Australia and New Zealand, and Europe.

Barahona Center for the Study of Books in Spanish for Children and Adolescents (*www.csusm.edu/csb/English*).—Sponsored by California State University San Marcos, the Barahona Center is a database of Spanish books for children and adolescents. The database allows the user to search by age, subject, grade, setting, publisher or publication date, and reviewer. Recommended lists and special lists of award-winning books that have been translated into Spanish are available.

Oyate (*www.oyate.org*).—Oyate is a Native American organization that works to ensure that the lives and histories of native peoples are portrayed honestly. Oyate's work includes evaluation of texts, resource materials, and fiction by and about native peoples.

Coretta Scott King Award (*www.ala.org*).—The Coretta Scott King Book Award is presented annually by the Coretta Scott King Committee of the American Library Association's Ethnic Multicultural Information Exchange Round Table (EMIERT). The award (or awards) is given to an African American author and an African American illustrator for an outstandingly inspirational and educational contribution. The books promote understanding and appreciation of the culture of all peoples and their contribution to the realization of the American dream.

The Pura Belpré Award (*www.ala.org/Template.cfm?Section=bookmediaawards&template=/ContentManagement/ContentDisplay.cfm&ContentID=102627*).—This award, established in 1996, is presented to a Latino/Latina writer and illustrator whose work best portrays, affirms, and celebrates the Latino cultural experience in an outstanding work of literature for children and youth.

Native Writers Circle of the Americas Award (*www.literature-awards.com/native_writers_circle.htm*).—These are the only literature awards bestowed on Native American Indian writers by Native American Indian people. The awards are given in three categories: Lifetime Achievement Awards; First Book Awards for Poetry; First Book Awards for Prose.

Américas Award (*www.uwm.edu/Dept/CLACS/outreach/americas.html*).—This award recognizes U.S. published works of fiction, poetry, folklore, or selected nonfiction for children and young adults that authentically and engagingly relate to Latin America, the Caribbean, or Latinos in the United States.

Tomas Rivera Mexican American Children's Book Award (*www.education.txstate.edu/ subpages/tomasrivera*).—This award is given annually to the author/illustrator of the most distinguished book for children and young adults that authentically reflects the lives and experiences of Mexican Americans in the United States.

Notable Books for a Global Society (NBGS) (*www.csulb.edu/org/childrens-lit/proj/ nbgs/intro-nbgs.html*).—Outstanding multicultural literature for pre-K through 12th-grade students.

Asian Pacific American Award for Literature (*www.apalaweb.org/awards/awards. htm*).—The Asian/Pacific American Librarians Association bestows this award for books by or about Asian Pacific Americans.

Children's Fiction Books for Fourth Grade

Alphin, E. M. (1996). *A bear for Miguel.* New York: HarperCollins.

Birdsall, J. (2005). *The Penderwicks: A summer tale of four sisters, two rabbits, and a very interesting boy.* New York: Knopf.

Blume, J. (1972). *Tales of a fourth grade nothing.* Illustrated by R. Doty. New York: Dutton.

Cole, J. (1986). *The magic school bus at the waterworks.* Illustrated by B. Degen. New York: Scholastic.

Curtis, C. P. (1999). *Bud, not Buddy.* New York: Delacorte Press.

DiCamillo, K. (2000). *Because of Winn-Dixie.* Cambridge, MA: Candlewick Press.

DiCamillo, K. (2006). *The miraculous journey of Edward Tulane.* Illustrated by B. Ibatuline. Cambridge, MA: Candlewick Press.

Gantos, J. (2000). *Joey Pigza loses control.* New York: Farrar, Straus & Giroux.

Gardiner, J. R. (1980). *Stone fox.* Illustrated by M. Sewall. New York: Crowell.

Giovanni, N. (2005). *Rosa.* Illustrated by B. Collier. New York: Holt.

Goble, P. (1978). *The girl who loved wild horses.* Scarsdale, NY: Bradbury Press.

Kelsey, E. (1998). *Finding out about whales.* Toronto: Owl.

Krull, K. (1996). *Wilma unlimited: How Wilma Rudolph became the world's fastest woman.* Illustrated by D. Diaz. San Diego, CA: Harcourt Brace.

Levine, A. (1994). *The boy who drew cats: A Japanese folktale.* Illustrated by F. Clement. New York: Dial Books for Young Readers.

Lewis, C. S. (1950). *The lion, the witch, and the wardrobe.* Illustrated by P. Baynes. New York: HarperCollins.

Lowry, L. (1989). *Number the stars.* Boston: Houghton Mifflin.

McMillian, B. (2005). *The problem with chickens.* Illustrated by Gunnella. Boston: Houghton Mifflin.

Myers, W. (2006). *Jazz*. Illustrated by C. Myers. New York: Holiday House.

Nye, N. S. (1994). *Sitti's secrets*. Illustrated by N. Carpenter. New York: Four Winds Press.

Rappaport, D. (2001). *Martin's big words*. Illustrated by B. Collier. New York: Hyperion.

Ryan, P. M. (2002). *When Marian sang*. Illustrations by B. Selznick. New York: Scholastic.

Scieszka, J. (1993). *The not-so-jolly roger*. Illustrated by L. Smith. New York: Puffin Books.

Sharmat, M. W. (1972). *Nate the great*. Illustrated by M. Simont. New York: Coward, McCann & Geoghegan.

Sidman, J. (2005). *The song of the water boatman and other pond poems*. Illustrated by B. Prange. Boston: Houghton Mifflin.

Soto, G. (2005). *Worlds apart: Fernie and me*. New York: Putnam.

Steptoe, J. (1987). *Mufaro's beautiful daughters: An African tale*. New York: Lothrop, Lee & Shepard Books.

Van Allsburg, C. (1990). *Just a dream*. Boston: Houghton Mifflin.

Woodson, J. (2005). *Show way*. Illustrated by H. Talbott. New York: Putnam.

Young, J. (2006). *R is for rhyme: A poetry alphabet*. Chelsea, MI: Sleeping Bear Press.

Children's Nonfiction for Fourth Grade

Aldrin, B., & Minor, W. (2005). *Buzz Aldrin: Reaching for the moon*. New York: HarperCollins.

Armstrong, J. (2000). *Shipwreck at the bottom of the world: The extraordinary true story of Shackleton and the Endurance*. New York: Crown.

Armstrong, J. (2006). *The American story*. New York: Holiday House.

Bardoe, C. (2006). *Gregor Mendel: The friar who grew peas*. New York: Abrams.

Bledsoe, L. (2006). *How to survive Antarctica*. New York: Holiday House.

Blumberg, R. (2001). *Shihpwrecked!* New York: HarperCollins.

Blumenthal, K. (2005). *Let me play: The story of Title IX: The law that changed the future of girls in America*. New York: Atheneum.

Burleigh, R. (1998). *Black whiteness: Admiral Byrd alone in the Antarctic*. Illustrated by W. Krudop. New York: Atheneum.

Burleigh, R. (2006). *Paul Cezanne: A painter's journey*. New York: Abrams.

Canales, V. (2005). *The tequila worm*. New York: Wendy Lamb.

Cherry, L. (1990). *The great kapok tree*. San Diego, CA: Harcourt Brace Jovanovich.

Danenberg, B. (2005). *Shadow life*. New York: Scholastic.

Davies, N. (2006). *Extreme animals: The toughest creatures on earth*. Cambridge, MA: Candlewick Press.

Demi. (2006). *Su Dongpo: Chinese genius*. New York: Lee & Low.

Dennis, Y. W., & Hirschfelder, A. (2003). *Children of Native America today*. Watertown, MA: Charlesbridge.

Edwards, P. (2005). *The bus ride that changed history*. Boston: Houghton Mifflin.

Ellabbad, M. (2006). *The illustrator's notebook*. Toronto: Groundwood Books.

Fleischman, J. (2002). *Phineas Gage*. Boston: Houghton Mifflin.

Freedman, R. (1987). *Lincoln: A photobiography*. Boston: Houghton Mifflin.

Freedman, R. (2004). *The voice that challenged a nation: Marian Anderson and the struggle for equal rights*. Boston: Houghton Mifflin

Freedman, R. (2006). *The adventures of Marco Polo*. New York: Levine.

Freedman, R. (2006). *Freedom walkers*. Boston: Houghton Mifflin.

Freeman, D. (2003). *How people live*. New York: DK Publishing.

Fritz, J. (2007). *Who's saying what in Jamestown, Thomas Savage?* New York: Putnam.

Gerstein, M. (2003). *The man who walked between the towers*. Brookfield, CT: Roaring Brook Press.

Giblin, J. (2005). *Good brother, bad brother*. Boston: Houghton Mifflin.

Goldstone, B. (2006). *Great estimations*. New York: Holt.

Hopkinson, D. (1999). *Maria's comet*. New York: Atheneum.

Jenkins, S. (2006). *Almost gone: The world's rarest animals*. New York: Harper-Collins.

Jurmain, S. (2005). *George did it*. New York: Dutton.

Kroll, V. (2006). *Selvakumar knew better*. Freemont, CA: Shen's Books.

Krull, K. (2003). *Harvesting hope: The story of Caesar Chavez*. San Diego, CA: Harcourt.

Langone, J. (2004). *New how things work*. Washington, DC: National Geographic Society.

Levine, E. (2000). *Darkness over Denmark*. New York: Holiday House.

Levinson, N. (1992). *Snowshoe Thompson*. New York: HarperCollins.

Lin, G. (2006). *Our seasons*. Watertown, MA: Charlesbridge.

Macaulay, D. (1977). *Castle*. Boston: Houghton Mifflin.

Macaulay, D. (2000). *Building*. Boston: Houghton Mifflin.

Macy, S. (2006). *Freeze frame: A photographic history of the Winter Olympics.* Washington, DC: National Geographic Society.

Martin, J. (1998). *Snowflake Bentley.* Boston: Houghton Mifflin.

McCully, E. (2006). *Marvelous Mattie: How Margret E. Knight became an inventor.* New York: Farrar, Straus & Giroux.

McLeod, S. (2005). *Dare to dream!: 25 lives of extraordinary people.* Buffalo, NY: Prometheus.

Montgomery, S. (2004). *The tarantula scientist.* Boston: Houghton Mifflin.

Nelson, S. (2006). *Quiet hero: The Ira Hayes story.* New York: Lee & Low.

Newquist, H. (2005). *The great brain book.* New York: Scholastic.

Nikola-Lisa, W. (2006). *How smart are we.* New York: Lee & Low.

Paulsen, G. (2001). *Guts.* New York: Delacourt.

Piven, H. (2006). *What athletes are made of.* New York: Atheneum.

Pringle, L. (2006). *American slave, American hero: York of the Lewis and Clarke expedition.* Honesdale, PA: Calkins Creek.

Rappaport, D. (2006). *Nobody gonna turn me 'round.* Cambridge, MA: Candlewick Press.

Reynolds, J. (2006). *Celebrate connections among cultures.* New York: Lee & Low.

Simon, S. (2002). *Destination: Space.* New York: HarperCollins.

Sousa, J. (2006). *Faces, places, and inner spaces.* New York: Abrams.

St. George, J. (2002). *So you want to be an inventor?* New York: Philomel.

Stewart, M. (2006). *A place for butterflies.* Atlanta, GA: Peachtree.

Tang, G. (2003). *Math-terpieces: The art of problem-solving.* New York: Scholastic.

Thimmesh, C. (2004). *Madam President: The extraordinary, true (and evolving) story of women in politics.* Boston: Houghton Mifflin.

Thimmesh, C. (2006). *Team moon: How 400,000 people landed Apollo 11 on the moon.* Boston: Houghton Mifflin.

Thomas, J. (2003). *Linda Brown, you are not alone.* New York: Jump at the Sun/Hyperion.

Turck, M. (2004). *Mexico and Central America: A fiesta of cultures.* Chicago Review Press.

Wang, X. (2006). *One year in Beijing.* New York: Chinasprout.

Webb, S. (2000). *My season with penguins.* Boston: Houghton Mifflin.

Weber, E. (2004). *Rattlesnake Mesa.* New York: Lee & Low.

Winter, J. (2004). *Calavera Abecedario: A Day of the Dead alphabet.* San Diego, CA: Harcourt.

Winter, J. (2006). *Dizzy*. New York: Levine.

Wolf, B. (2003). *Coming to America: A Muslim family story*. New York: Lee & Low.

Yolen, J., & Stemple, H. (1999). *The Mary Celeste: A mystery from history*. New York: Simon & Schuster.

Supplemental Materials for Content-Area Instruction

➤ New Bridge Nonfiction Guided Reading and Writing (*www.newbridgeonline.com*)

➤ National Geographic content-area reading, leveled texts, and themed sets (*www.ngschoolpub.org*)

➤ Tony Stead Science and Social Studies Content-Area Collections by Rosen Publishing (*www.rosenclassroom.com*)

➤ Scholastic Guided Reading Programs, developed by Gay Su Pinnell, in content-area reading, nonfiction, fiction, and *en español* (*www.teacher.scholastic.com*)

➤ Learning Media nonfiction shared reading (*www.nelsoned.com*)

➤ Primary source readers by Teacher Created Materials (*www.teachercreatedmaterials.com*)

PROFESSIONAL DEVELOPMENT RESOURCES

It is incredibly important for teachers to continue to grow by learning, not only because it mirrors what they are asking their students do, but because effective teachers constantly evaluate the strategies they use and how successful their teaching is in order to create an optimum learning environment and meet all students' needs. The following list provides resources in a variety of areas important to effective literacy instruction.

Instructional Practices

Allington, R. L., & Johnston, P. N. (2002). *Reading to learn: Lessons from exemplary fourth-grade classrooms*. New York: Guilford Press.

Fountas, I., & Pinnell, G. (2002). *Guiding readers and writers grades 3–6*. Portsmouth, NH: Heinemann.

Fountas, I., & Pinnell, G. (2006). *Teaching for comprehension and fluency: Thinking, talking, and writing about reading, K–8*. Portsmouth, NH: Heinemann.

Johnston, P. (2004). *Choice words: How our language affects children's learning*. Portland, ME: Stenhouse.

Lesene, T. (2003). *Making the match: The right book for the right reader at the right time, grades 4–12*. Portland, ME: Stenhouse.

Routman, R. (2003). *Reading essentials: The specifics you need to teach reading well*. Portsmouth, NH: Heinemann.

Sibberson, F., & Szymusiak, K. (2003). *Still learning to read: Teaching students in grades 3–6*. Portland, ME: Stenhouse.

Szymusiak, K., & Sibberson, F. (2001). *Beyond leveled books: Supporting transitional readers in grades 2–5*. Portland, ME: Stenhouse.

The Literacy Project (*www.google.com/literacy*).—A search engine designed as a resource for teachers, literacy organizations, and anyone interested in reading and education. Find books, articles, and videos about literacy, or start your own literacy or reading group!

Literacy Connections (*www.literacyconnections.com/index.html*).—A website dedicated to reading, teaching, and tutoring techniques, ESL literacy, and adult literacy. Topics include the language experience approach, phonics, word study, and the best in children's literature.

Assessment

Beaver, J. (2003). *Developmental reading assessment* (2nd ed., grades 4–8). New York: Pearson Learning.

Caldwell, J., & Leslie, L. (2005). *Intervention strategies to follow informal reading inventory assessment: So what do I do now?* Boston: Allyn & Bacon.

Flynt, D., Flynt, E., & Cooter, R. (2004). *Flynt–Cooter Reading Inventory for the classroom* (5th ed.). Upper Saddle River, NJ: Merrill.

Ruiz, O., & Cuesta, V. (n.d.) *Evaluacion Del Desarrollo De La Lectura* [Assessment for Spanish-speaking students] *K–6*. New York: Pearson Learning.

Shea, M. (2006). *Where's the Glitch?: How to use running records with older readers*. Portsmouth, NH: Heinemann.

Strickland, K. (2005). *What's after assessment?: Follow-up instruction for phonics, fluency, and comprehension*. Portsmouth, NH: Heinemann.

Reading Aloud

Hahn, M. (2002). *Reconsidering read-aloud*. Portland, ME: Stenhouse.

Laminack, L., & Wadsworth, R. (2006). *Reading aloud across the curriculum*. Portsmouth, NH: Heinemann.

Serafini, F., & Giorgis, C. (2003). *Reading aloud and beyond: Fostering the intellectual life with older readers*. Portsmouth, NH: Heinemann.

Shared and Guided Reading

Allen, J. (2002). *On the same page: Shared reading beyond the primary grades*. Portland, ME: Stenhouse.

Opitz, M., & Ford, M. (2001). *Reaching readers: Flexible and innovative strategies for guided reading*. Portsmouth, NH: Heinemann.

Schulman, M. (2006). *Guided reading in grades 3–6*. New York: Scholastic.

Vocabulary and Word Study

Allen, J. (2007). *Inside words: Tools for teaching academic vocabulary, grades 4–12*. Portland, ME: Stenhouse.

Bear, D., Invernizzi, M., Templeton, S., & Johnston, F. (2008) *Words their way: Word study for phonics, vocabulary, and spelling instruction* (4th ed.). Upper Saddle River, NJ: Merrill.

Beck, I., McKeown, M., & Kucan, L. (2002). *Bringing words to life: Robust vocabulary instruction*. New York: Guilford Press.

Ganske, K. (2000). *Word journeys: Assessment-guided phonics, spelling, and vocabulary instruction*. New York: Guilford Press.

Fluency

Opitz, M., & Rasinski, T. (1998). *Good-bye round robin*. Portsmouth, NH: Heinemann.

Prescott-Griffin, M., & Witherell, N. (2004). *Fluency in focus: Comprehension strategies for all young readers*. Portsmouth, NH: Heinemann.

Shepard, A. (2005). *Stories on stage: Children's plays for Reader's Theater (or Readers' Theatre), with 15 play scripts from 15 authors, including Roald Dahl's* The Twits *and Louis Sachar's* Sideways Stories from Wayside School. Olympia, WA: Shepard.

Worthy, J. (2005). *Readers theater for building fluency: Strategies and scripts for making the most of this highly effective, motivating, and research-based approach to oral reading, grades 3–6*. New York: Scholastic.

Comprehension

Beck, I., McKeown, M., Hamilton, R., & Kucan, L. (1997). *Questioning the author: An approach for enhancing student engagement with text*. Newark, DE: International Reading Association.

Dorn, L., & Soffas, C. (2005). *Teaching for deep comprehension: A reading workshop approach*. Portland, ME: Stenhouse.

Harvey, S., & Goudvis, A. (2007). *Strategies that work* (2nd ed.). Portland, ME: Stenhouse.

Keene, E., & Zimmerman, S. (2007). *Mosaic of thought: The power of comprehension strategy instruction* (2nd ed.). Portsmouth, NH: Heinemann.

McLaughlin, M., & Allen, M. (2002). *Guided comprehension in action: Lessons for grades 3–8*. Newark, DE: International Reading Association.

Sarafini, F. (2004). *Lessons in comprehension: Explicit instruction in the reading workshop*. Portsmouth, NH: Heinemann.

Wilhelm, J. (2001). *Improving comprehension with think-aloud strategies: Modeling what good readers do*. New York: Scholastic.

Reading Rockets: Comprehension 101 (*www.readingrockets.org/teaching/reading101/comprehension*).—This site offers a short videoclip on reciprocal teaching, a teaching routine that assists children in orchestrating the use of comprehension strategies when reading. Also, several excellent articles are available.

Literature Discussion

Cole, A. (2003). *Knee to knee, eye to eye: Circling in on comprehension*. Portsmouth, NH: Heinemann.

Johnson, H., & Freedman, L. (2005). *Content area literature circles: Using discussion for learning across the curriculum*. Norwood, MA: Christopher-Gordon.

Nichols, M. (2006). *Comprehension through conversation: The power of purposeful talk in the reading workshop*. Portsmouth, NH: Heinemann.

Ciritcal Thinking

Cowhey, M. (2006). *Black ants and Buddists: Thinking critically and teaching differently in the primary grades*. Portland, ME: Stenhouse.

Dozier, C., Johnston, P., & Rogers, R. (2006). *Critical literacy, critical teaching: Tools for preparing responsive teachers*. New York: Teachers College Press.

Grammar

Anderson, J. (2005). *Mechanically inclined: Building grammar, usage, and style into writer's workshop*. Portland, ME: Stenhouse.

Weaver, C. (1996). *Teaching grammar in context*. Portsmouth, NH: Heinemann.

Writing

Cruz, M. (2004). *Independent writing: One teacher—thirty-two needs, topics, and plans*. Portsmouth, NH: Heinemann.

Dorfman, L., & Cappelli, R. (2007). *Mentor texts: Teaching writing through children's literature*. Portland, ME: Stenhouse.

Portalupi, J., & Fletcher, R. (2001). *Nonfiction craft lessons: Teaching information writing K–8*. Portland, ME: Stenhouse.

Ray, K. (2006). *Study driven: A framework for planning units of study in the writing workshop.* Portsmouth, NH: Heinemann.

Routman, R. (2005). *Writing essentials: Raising expectations and results while simplifying teaching.* Portsmouth, NH: Heinemann.

Inside Writing Communities 3–5 (learner.org/resources/series205.html).—A video workshop for grades 3–5 teachers that uses classroom footage to demonstrate how a writing workshop approach motivates intermediate students and helps them become proficient and independent writers.

English Language Learners

Bear, D., Helman, L., Templeton, S., Invernizzi, M., & Johnston, F. (2007) *Words their way with English learners.* Upper Saddle River, NJ: Merrill.

Cary, S. (2004). *Going graphic: Comics in the multilingual classroom.* Portsmouth, NH: Heinemann.

Fay, K., & Whaley, S. (2004). *Becoming one community: Reading and writing with English language learners.* Portland, ME: Stenhouse.

Fitzgerald, J., & Graves, M. (2004). *Scaffolding reading experiences for English-language learners.* Norwood, MA: Christopher Gordon.

Kendall, J., & Khuon, K. (2005). *Making sense: Small-group comprehension lessons for English language learners.* Portland, ME: Stenhouse.

Reid, S. (2002). *Book bridges for ESL students: Using young adult and children's literature to teach ESL.* Lanham, MD: Scarecrow Press.

Van Sluys, K. (2005). *What if and why?: Literacy invitations for multilingual classrooms.* Portsmouth, NH: Heinemann.

Family Literacy

Hull, G., & Schultz, K. (Eds.). (2002). *School's out!: Bridging out-of-school literacies with classroom practice.* New York: Teachers College, Columbia University.

Lilly, E., & Green, C. (2004). *Developing partnerships with families through children's literature.* Upper Saddle River, NJ: Merrill.

Tween Literacy

Beamon, G. (1997). *Sparking the thinking of students, ages 10–14: Strategies for teachers.* Thousand Oaks, CA: Corwin Press.

Lesene, T. (2006). *Naked reading: Uncovering what tweens need to become lifelong readers.* Portland, ME: Stenhouse.

Morgan, B. (2005). *Writing through tween years: Supporting writers, grades 3–6.* Portland, ME: Stenhouse.

Struggling Readers

Allington, R. (2006). *What really matters for struggling readers: Designing research-based programs* (2nd ed.). Boston: Allyn & Bacon.

Johnson, P. (2006). *One child at a time: Making the most of your time with struggling readers, K–6.* Portland, ME: Stenhouse.

McCormack, R., & Paratore, J. (Eds.). (2003). *After early intervention, then what?: Teaching struggling readers in grades 3 and beyond.* Newark, DE: International Reading Association.

Strickland, D., & Alvermann, D. (Eds.). (2004). *Bridging the literacy achievement gap: Grades 4–12.* New York: Teachers College, Columbia University.

Students with Disabilities

Center for Applied Special Technology (CAST; www.cast.org).—CAST is a nonprofit organization that works to expand learning opportunities for all individuals, especially those with disabilities, through the research and development of innovative, technology-based educational resources and strategies.

The Schneider Family Book Awards (www.ala.org).—These awards honor an author or illustrator for a book that embodies an artistic expression of the disability experience for child and adolescent audiences. Three awards are given annually in each of the following categories: birth through grade school (ages 0–10 years), middle school (ages 11–13), and teens (age 13–18). The book must emphasize an artistic expression of the disability experience for children or adolescent audiences. The book must portray some aspect of living with a disability, or that of a friend or family member, whether the disability is physical, mental, or emotional.

Technology Integration

Cummins, J., Brown, K., & Sayers, D. (2007). *Literacy, technology, and diversity: Teaching for success in changing times.* Boston: Allyn & Bacon.

Eagleton, M. B., & Dobler, E. (2007). *Reading the web: Strategies for Internet inquiry.* New York: Guilford Press.

Karchmer, R., Mallette, M., Kara-soteriou, J., & Leu, D. (Eds.). (2005). *Innovative approaches to literacy education: Using the Internet to support new literacies.* Newark, DE: International Reading Association.

Labbo, L., Love, M., Prior, M., Hubbard, B., & Ryan, T. (2006). *Literature links: Thematic units linking read-alouds and computer activities.* Newark, DE: International Reading Association.

Wood, J. (2004). *Literacy online: New tools for struggling readers and writers.* Portsmouth, NH: Heinemann.

Integrating Literacy and Technology in the Curriculum: A position statement by the International Reading Association (*www.reading.org/resources/issues/positions_technology.html*).

The International Reading Association's resources in technology (*www.reading.org/resources/issues/focus_technology.html*).—This website has a listing of resources on the use of technology in teaching literacy.

The National Council of Teachers of English's Reading and Writing on the Web (*www.ncte.org/collections/weblit*).—A collection of resources for reading and writing on the Web.

The New Literacies Research Team (*www.newliteracies.uconn.edu*).—The New Literacies Research Team at the University of Connecticut is a continually evolving consortium of professors, graduate researchers, school districts, organizations, policymakers, teachers, and school leaders who seek to prepare students for the new learning and literacy skills required by information and communication technologies such as the Internet.

The National Center for Technology Innovation's Reading Matrix (*www. nationaltechcenter. org/matrix/default.asp#*).—Outlines six purposes of technology that support reading for students with special needs.

Literacy and Technology Integration (*www.literacy.uconn.edu/littech.htm*).—Hosted by the University of Connecticut, this site has an extensive annotated list of links to sites that provide examples of learning literacy with technology and sites devoted to integrating technology.

Motivation and Engagement

Baker, L., Dreher, M. J., & Guthrie, J. T. (2000). *Engaging young readers: Promoting achievement and motivation.* New York: Guilford Press.

Contexts for Engagement and Motivation in Reading by John T. Guthrie (*www. readingonline.org/articles/handbook/guthrie*).—This article focuses on the instructional contexts that promote student motivation and engaged reading and the consequences of that engagement in what is read.

Content-Area Instruction

Daniels, H., & Zemelman, S. (2004). *Subjects matter: Every teacher's guide to content-area reading.* Portsmouth, NH: Heinemann.

McKee, J., & Ogle, D. (2005). *Integrating instruction: Literacy and science.* New York: Guilford Press.

National Council for the Social Studies (NCSS) Notable Books (*www.socialstudies.org/resources/notable*).—The books that appear in these annotated book lists were evaluated and selected by a book review committee appointed by the NCSS and assembled in cooperation with the Children's Book Council (CBC). NCSS and CBC have cooperated on this annual bibliography since 1972. Books selected for this bibliography are written primarily for children in grades K–8. The selection committee looks for books that emphasize human relations, represent a diversity of groups and are sensitive to a broad range of cultural experiences, present an original theme or a fresh slant on a traditional topic, are easily readable and of high literary quality, and have a pleasing format and, when appropriate, illustrations that enrich the text. Each book is read by several reviewers, and books are included on the list by committee assent; annotations do not necessarily reflect the judgment of the entire committee.

National Association of Science Teachers: Outstanding Science Trade Books for Students K–12 (www.nsta.org/ostbc).—Since 1973, the review panel of the National Science Teachers Association, in cooperation with the Children's Book Council, has selected the Outstanding Science Trade Books for Children. The panel uses rigorous selection guidelines relating to the presentation of material.

INDEX

Page numbers followed by *f* indicate figure, *t* indicate table